Voices of Islam

By the same author:

VOICES
OF ISLAM

JOHN BOWKER

ONEWORLD
OXFORD

VOICES OF ISLAM

Oneworld Publications
(Sales and Editorial)
185 Banbury Road
Oxford OX2 7AR
England

Oneworld Publications
(US Marketing Office)
42 Broadway
Rockport, MA 01966
USA

ISBN 1–85168–095–0

Printed and bound by
WSOY, Finland

Contents

CHAPTER 3:

MUSLIMS AND NON-MUSLIMS: THE STATE AND HOLY WAR, OTHER RELIGIONS, APOSTASY AND TREASON

CHAPTER 4:

THE NATURE OF WOMEN AND THEIR STATUS

CHAPTER 5:

EDUCATION AND FREEDOM OF ENQUIRY

Preface

The publication of the novel *The Satanic Verses* evoked anger and hostility in the Muslim world, but it evoked anger and hostility in the non-Muslim world as well. Islam was accused of being intolerant, of being fundamentalist and fanatical, and of being frozen in a past in which those who offended by writing unacceptable books might be executed. But now? How can burning a book and seeking to kill its author be reconciled with freedom of speech? This anger has been powerfully reinforced by a perception of Muslims as people who subordinate women to men, stone adulterers to death, cut off the hands of thieves, execute anyone who apostatizes Islam, and who seek to conquer or convert all those with whom they disagree. Those, at least, were the opinions of Islam which were commonly heard at the time.

It was in this context that the BBC World Service decided to make a series of programmes on 'what Muslims really believe'. The programmes began with the expression of exactly those opinions of Islam, in no uncertain terms. They then focused on interviews with Muslims, drawn from different parts of the wide spectrum of Islam, responding to those criticisms and questions. This book is based on the programmes, but it contains much more material than it was possible to include in the series. It consists almost entirely of transcripts of the interviews. I have made no attempt to alter the original words, and although this makes for harder reading in some respects, it nevertheless remains faithful to the original intention of listening to Muslims giving their own account, in their own words, of what Islam means for them. The book concentrates on the issues which, in the non-Muslim, evoke fear and suspicion or, like those just mentioned, create the impression that Islam is a fanatical threat to human rights and freedoms. It is not an encyclopaedia of Islamic belief in all its manifestations.

For those who wish to go further, I would commend M. A. Quasem's *Salvation of the Soul and Islamic Devotions* (London: Kegan Paul International, 1983), Y. al-Qaradawi's *Al-Halal wal-Haram fil-Islam* (translated as *The Lawful and the Prohibited in Islam*, Indianapolis: American Trust Publications, n.d.), and on a specific issue of great importance in understanding Islam in the world, A. R. I. Doi's, *Non-Muslims under Sharia (Islamic Law)* (London: Ta Ha Publishers, 1983). The Muslim understanding of wider and more general issues will be found in my own *Worlds of Faith: Religions in the UK Today*, which was also based on interviews for a BBC series. There are several English versions of the Qur'ān (the Muslim holy book), none really satisfactory. The Muslim recommendation is to learn Arabic. There is no standard or agreed numbering of the verses of the Qur'ān (hence some of the references in this book give the alternative possibilities). The renderings in English are my own.

In general, terms such as Sharia have been given in forms which assimilate them to English, and not in strict transliteration from the Arabic; the transliterated forms will be found in the glossary. Equally, it should be borne in mind that Muslims, on each occasion that the name of the Prophet Muḥammad is mentioned, repeat the prayer, 'May God's peace and blessing be upon him'. Sometimes in English books, this is represented by the initials P.B.U.H.; in this book, after consultation, it was decided that this would be intrusive for the non-Muslim reader, and it has been omitted in the text. It cannot ever be omitted from the heart of the Muslim.

The series owes everything to David Craig, its producer, and as always I have learned much from him and his commitment to religious broadcasting, to making it genuinely religious. I am grateful for the opportunity to work with him again, and I am equally grateful to Margaret, my wife, who yet again allowed the chance of a holiday that year to disappear into the making of the programmes. And above all, I am grateful to those who agreed to talk with such honesty and integrity about their understanding of Islam. The contributors, both men and women, ranged from highly trained academics to those pursuing a range of different jobs in the community at large. As they themselves make clear, there cannot be one, single voice of Islam. Islam insists and depends on diversity of interpretation and debate. Thus none of them can speak for any but themselves. We have tried to include a representation of the many different styles of Islam, and I have not tried to adjudicate between them when they disagree. But what is clear from the programmes and the book is . . . But for that, perhaps the book should speak for itself.

CHAPTER ONE

AUTHORITY AND COMMUNITY:
REVELATION, THE QUR'ĀN AND THE FOUNDATIONS OF ISLAM

Attitudes to Islam

About a quarter of the entire population of the world lives in China – something like a thousand million people. And that figure is also approximately the number of Muslims in the world. Muslims are mainly concentrated in a swathe of countries running from North Africa to Indonesia and the Philippines, but they are to be found in virtually every country. In China itself the Muslim population could be (exact figures are not available) something like half the population of England.

These are large numbers, and the point of making these comparisons is simply to emphasize how extensive the fact of Islam is. Of the world religions, only Christianity is larger. Not surprisingly, the world of Islam is constantly in the news: protests over Salman Rushdie's novel *The Satanic Verses;* the division of Cyprus; the conflict in the Lebanon; the Palestinian *intifada;* Iran and Iraq; Algeria; the *mujahidun* in Afghanistan; the search for identity and statehood among the extensive Muslim populations of the former USSR; Pakistan and India; the separatist movements in South-East Asia; the Sudan.

But all these examples are examples also of conflict. They have helped to create an impression of Islam as threatening and coercive. In preparation for the programmes on the World Service, we asked people at random, in different parts of Europe, what they thought of Islam. The answers were strong, to say the least:

'I find their religion very aggressive. If I had to deal with them I would be very, very careful.'

'It's the culture I object to mainly, with the woman in the traditional role, as we see it, or worse, being forced into a way of life where even the clothing that they wear is specified by the religion, by the culture.'

'They are inclined to be very aggressive in the defence of what they think and what they believe.'

'I regard it as a very bigoted religion, even more bigoted than established Christianity.'

'They don't belong to Europe, because we are Christians, and Muslims shouldn't be here.'

'The Muslim religion is very good for desert countries, but not for Europe, not for a northern climate.'

'They are very aggressive: they burn books, they attack people, they don't tolerate other people.'

Impressionistic, to say the least. It adds up to one word, which occurs more than any other when people try to summarize what they know about Islam: fanaticism. Many people perceive Islam as a threat, and there is nothing new in that perception, at least in Europe. Within a hundred years of the death of the prophet Muhammad (from whose faithful transmission of the word of God, according to Islamic belief, in the sixth century of the Christian era, Islam takes its beginning), Islam had extended from the Atlantic coast of North Africa to the borders of China. This was partly through the simplicity and attractiveness of the message, partly through trade and partly through conquest. It was the conquest which Europe noted.

Before long Muslims were ruling in Spain, in 1453 Constantinople fell, and, not long after, Muslim armies were at the gates of Vienna. The best that people could then find to say of Islam (and Luther did say it) was that Islam was an instrument used by God to punish Christians for their faithless ways. The worst that could be said was much more frequently said, as by Humphrey Prideaux, a Dean of Norwich in the late seventeenth century. He entitled his widely read 'life of Mahomet' *The True Nature of Imposture Fully Displayed*. He claimed of Islam:

> Where the religion is all forgery and falsehood . . . deceit and fraud, the imposture then becomes so totally and perfectly wicked, without the least mixture of good therein, as must necessarily denominate the authors and first propagators of it to be perfectly wicked also.

The negative opinion of Islam is no new thing. It is true that during the nineteenth century there were some who made an attempt to give a more informed account, so that when Carlyle wrote *Heroes and Hero-Worship*, he could choose for his example of the Hero as Prophet, not Isaiah or Jeremiah, nor even John the Baptist, but Muḥammad. Carlyle admired the sincerity of the Qur'ān and the simplicity of Muslim beliefs. He admired even more the fact that what Muslims believe 'with wild rapt earnestness' they also consistently practise:

> Belief is great, life-giving . . . These Arabs, the man Mahomet, and that one century – it is as if a spark had fallen, one spark, on a world of what seemed black, unnoticeable sand, but lo, the sand proves explosive powder, blazes high from Delhi to Granada! I said, the Great Man was always as lightning out of Heaven; the rest

of men waited for him like fuel, and then they too would flame.

But there we are again! Even Carlyle's relatively approving account ends on a note of fire and fury – the same note that we are still hearing now:

'They are fanatics. The women are still without rights.'

'They frighten men, because they can be violent.'

'They're violent, they're brutal: they're kidnappers, book-burners.'

'They just have children in order to become strong. They will be very dangerous, if they are coming here to live and are going to be accepted in Europe. After a hundred years we would no longer be Europeans, because we would be overloaded with Muslims.'

'They are cunning, they cheat, they fight. In a dispute even over twenty-five cents, they might try to kill someone, but not openly – they would kill from behind. They are a very big threat to Europe.'

'I find their religion very aggressive. The women are without any rights. And they don't want to mix with anyone, they just stick together.'

But how has all this fear and prejudice come about? Consider what the word *islam* means: 'Islam from its root means "peace", and peace in such a way that people do seek understanding.' The underlying Arabic root *slm* underlies also the Hebrew word (and greeting) *shalom*. Islam means basically 'entering into a condition of peace and security through allegiance to God'.

Community and Peace

The purpose of that allegiance is to do the will of God and to restore the intention of God's creation by creating a single human community, unified in that condition of *islam*. That vision of a single community is summarized in the word *umma*. It is a vision of a single human family, deriving its life and guidance from God, and returning its life and obedience to Him. 'People were a single umma', says the Qur'ān (x. 19), but they have disrupted that single intended community into many rival *umam*, communities in a rebellious plurality: 'Then they fell into variance.' The purpose of Islam is to restore that community on the earth. Thus Islam is not an assembly of United Nations, it is a United Nation. The metaphysical nation, the umma, transcends the boundaries of nation-states. And however much the political realities at present contradict that, many Muslims experience Islam as exactly that:

'We are very united as far as our worship is concerned and as far as our daily life is concerned: you go into a mosque anywhere in the world and you will be able to pray, with everyone praying in exactly the same way that you are. I've travelled round countries like Spain, where the people are very different, but when you go to the mosque, you feel that they are brothers and sisters. It's a wonderful feeling, and I've found it throughout the world. At that level we are united, we are an umma, but at the political level – there's no doubt about it – we are fragmented.'

'The brotherhood of Muslims is something that one is aware of, travelling in the Muslim world as a Muslim, regardless of political differences; and I think that perhaps in the future our feeling of fellowship, which is strongest when we all pray facing to the one point of Mecca (which symbolizes our spiritual convergence from all points of the globe), will develop into a symbol of political and economic co-operation.'

No Compulsion in Religion

Far from being fanatical and seeking to force all others to become Muslim, Muslims insist (because the Qur'ān insists – ii. 256/7), that there is no compulsion in religion:

'I must make it absolutely clear that there is no compulsion to become a Muslim. The Qur'ānic *aya* [verse] says that there is no force – you cannot force an individual to become a Muslim. And I must tell you, if you look at the Islamic countries, even in Saudi Arabia, Iran, Turkey and other Muslim countries which have been Muslim for the last fourteen hundred years, there are still non-Muslim communities: there are Sikhs, Hindus, Christians, who have been living there for centuries and centuries. There are Jewish populations, and they are as happy as anybody else. So if there was forced conversion, then in the last fourteen hundred years they would have been converted to Islam. Muslims do not force individuals to accept the Faith, and therefore whoever is implying that you must cut throats to make someone do that, it's unIslamic and there is no justification for that whatsoever.'

According to the Qur'ān, to kill one is to kill all:

'Self-control is such a very great thing in the religion of Islam. One of the things that one is required to do in Islam is that when you are angry, you control yourself, you control your anger – you don't respond instinctively. You see, man responds according to his instincts, mostly. The value of religion is to teach one's instincts to be more civil, to respond in a way that will keep the peace and will not be hurtful to a person who may not be as tolerant as yourself. In other words, someone comes up with some lunatic idea, and I get angry. I am required by Islam to control my anger, and then to argue the case on rational grounds. If the other person accepts my argument, fine, well and good. If he doesn't, then I'll say, you have your view and I have mine, and let's just forget the difference and try to establish good neighbourly relationships. In other words, do not raise your hand against me in anger, do not kill me, and I will not kill you; do not attack me, and I will not attack you. I've said my view, you've said your view, and may God help both of us.'

JB: 'But to the outsider the impression has been created that Muslims do kill people they disagree with.'

'When you say "Muslims", I hope you don't include me! Because I haven't killed anybody yet. You see, when you read in the Qur'ān that if you kill one man without a very good reason (and the good reason being that he killed somebody, or that someone is coming to attack you, wanting to kill you), then it's like you have killed the whole of humanity. That's how big the sin of killing another person is, in the sight of God. Killing another person is described unequivocally in the Qur'ān as sin that leads to hell. Now, how can anyone say convincingly that Muslims who kill other people (or other Muslims) are committing a righteous act rather than a very sinful act? Of course it's extremely sinful to kill another man if you disagree with his views.'

Muslims, therefore, insist that Islam is inclusive and tolerant.

'In Islam there is complete freedom to worship according to your system, whether you are an idol-worshipper, or whether you are worshipping as *ahl al-Kitab* [People of the Book], that is as a Christian or a Jew. You can have your churches, synagogues, temples, and you can worship according to your own pattern. Under Islamic law no one can interfere with their worship. The Qur'ān says very clearly, "Do not cast aspersions on their idols, because they will then cast aspersions on God."'

Certainly, much will turn on the meaning of the word

tolerance. But in some sense of that word, there is a self-contradiction in Islam if that accepting and supportive attitude is not expressed:

'I hate the word *tolerance*, because it has all sorts of patronizing implications to it. But there must be tolerance for other faiths. Islam is not an intolerant religion. We see that within the Qur'ān itself. There were battles even in the time of Muhammad between Muhammad and peoples of other faiths. There were political struggles. But in principle, the People of the Book (and the word "Book" can be very widely interpreted) are people whom we respect and give dignity to.'

How then has this immense gap opened up between the popular impression of Islam as violent and fanatically aggressive, and the claim of Muslims that Islam is a way of peace? What is the real nature of Islamic community? Does it have to be aggressive in relation to non-Muslims, as was claimed in those strong rejections of Islam earlier? What *do* Muslims really believe?

The Qur'ān, Tradition and Law

At the foundation of Muslim life lie the absolute assurance and simplicity of its belief and practice, which rest on the Qur'ān. All those speaking above about Islamic tolerance base their reply on what the Qur'ān requires of them, and it is the Qur'ān, however much it has to be interpreted, which creates the non-negotiable foundation of Muslim life.

The Qur'ān, in Muslim belief, is the revelation of God's word to Muhammad in Arabia in the sixth century of the Christian era. Muslims have a different dating system, numbering years AH, or 'after the Hijra', the move which Muhammad made in faith from Mecca to Medina (*al-Madinah*). Muhammad is only one among many prophets, including Moses and Jesus. That is why Jews and Christians are called People of the Book, because they too received through their prophets exactly the same revelation. But in the case of Muhammad, the word was faithfully received and transmitted, and it was accepted by the first people who became Muslims in a way that did not distort or corrupt that revelation for their own purposes. So the Qur'ān is the same in content whether it is transmitted through Moses or Jesus or any other prophet. But those earlier communities distorted the Qur'ān for their own purposes. Only in the Arab (or Arabic) case is the word preserved as God intended it to be.

So Muslim life and belief are based absolutely on the Qur'ān, but the Qur'ān does not deal specifically with every issue or question that might arise. Muhammad and his first companions are, therefore, regarded as the first living commentators on the Qur'ān, exemplifying what it means in practice. The stories of what they said and did are known as *ahadith*, or more often in English as Hadith. Hadith becomes the second (though less absolute) foundation of Islam. Not all of the very many Hadith are of equal value: it depends on what they say and on the chain of the transmitters of the story, and Muslims have devoted much effort to establishing the degrees of reliability for all Hadith. Together, the Qur'ān and Hadith create the Sunna.

The Sunna is the path, the way to be followed in the practice of Islam. Even so, there was – and still is – much room for interpretation. In the early centuries of Islam, different schools of interpretation emerged, which produced what is known as *shari'a*. The word Sharia means literally 'the well-worn path made by camels, leading to the watering place'. Thus Sharia is in effect the path or pattern which Muslims follow (or are legally obliged to follow) in their lives. Sunna (the Qur'ān plus

21

Hadith) issues in the applied and canonical schools of Sharia, and these form the foundation and pattern of Muslim lives:

The Sharia mistakenly has been defined as Islamic law. The Sharia actually means "the way to water". Just as water purifies and gives growth and development to all creation, so the Sharia gives growth to human relationships and to our development as trustees of God. The sourcebook of Islam is the Qur'ān, and the second source is the Sunna, the teachings of the Prophet Muḥammad, which is a prophetic interpretation of the Qur'ān. And then there are a number of legal schools which have extrapolated from those two sources.'

Those different schools of Sharia, applied as they are in different countries and communities, are themselves different in emphasis. Thus the Hanbalites are recognized as being more conservative and strict in their interpretations. Already, therefore, the simple unity of Islam is becoming blurred:

'Muslim scholars don't concur on every single matter. In the Sunni orthodox tradition, there are four different schools of law which can dissent and do dissent from each other on various matters. Nevertheless, they accept each other's orthodoxy. There is mutual acceptance. Traditionally we call it *baraqa*, a blessing, that there is this dissent and disagreement on various matters of law, which are nevertheless all orthodox opinions.'

Caliphs and Authority: Sunni and Shia

Within the boundary of umma, it is therefore possible to contain wide variations of practice and interpretation. But that unity is much more profoundly disturbed by an even more fundamental divide among Muslims over the continuing source of authority in the community today. This division, which may separate one country from another, goes back to the earliest days of Islam.

The name *Shi'a* comes from the Arabic *shi'atu 'Alī*, the party of 'Alī, those who support the claim of 'Alī. Shia Muslims believe that, when Muhammad died, his nearest blood-relative, his son-in-law 'Alī, should have succeeded him as leader or Caliph (the word *khalifa* means 'successor' or 'representative'). He succeeded him eventually, as fourth Caliph, but only after three other Caliphs (the Ar-Rashidun) had held power before him, having been chosen by an entirely different system for designating the worthiest leader. 'Alī's position was disputed, and he was eventually killed in battle with other Muslims, as was his son. Both of them therefore became prototypical martyrs for the Shiite community, and a willingness to die for the Faith became a characteristic mark of Shiite Islam, as it is today. But far more distinctive of Shia Muslims (since other Muslims also believe that those who die as martyrs for the Faith have privileged access to heaven) is their sense that they have leaders, or imams, who, when they have appeared, have had God-derived and God-related authority. The Sunni Muslims, who constitute the vast majority in Islam, do not accept that claim. An imam, for the Sunnis, is simply the man who leads the prayers in the mosque and may have roles in education and preaching. Their leaders and guides in religious matters are the *'ulama*, the learned, who interpret Sharia and the Qur'ān. Neither they nor anyone else has absolute authority.

'If I speak of Islam, I can only speak for myself. To claim that I know authoritatively what is Islam is rather too arrogant. I have always criticized many of our people, or so-called religious leaders, for making such claims for themselves. In Islam we always say *"wa-Allahu 'alam"* after every statement – "God knows best" – and this is not simply an expression of humility, but an expression of a fundamental truth for a Muslim. We know what we have been told, and when we express our knowledge we express it with the limitations of being human beings, telling the people that this is our view. We are not compelling anyone to follow us. I am saying that this is what *I* believe. This is what I want to emphasize, that I keep saying to our leaders that they must avoid claiming that they are spokesmen of God. They are the interpreters of God's will. No one could make that other tremendous claim, without making a claim to direct communication with God, which is, in Islam, a privilege of the Prophet.'

JB: 'The outsider, though, has the impression that the Shiite understanding of the imam gives the imam a much stronger authority.'

'But the imams who have such authority are only twelve. Eleven of them have died, and one has disappeared and is awaited. That is the belief of the sect that prevails in Iran. The communication with God is therefore in the hand of a non-visible individual, the absent imam. But the ordinary *mujtahid*, the ordinary ayatollah, cannot and will not claim that he has communication with God. He would be violating the very principles of Shiism itself.'

JB: 'So his decisions are human decisions, human interpretations?'

'Indeed, indeed. That is the one characteristic of Shia *fiqh* or Shia law, that the leaders there, who are called *mujtahid* (that is, people who are using their opinions), are seeking after knowledge, and they therefore have more flexibility than many people realize.'

JB: 'But could an ordinary Muslim in Iran disagree with the decision of an ayatollah that Salman Rushdie should be executed? Is an ordinary Muslim able to disagree with and reject that?'

'Let me put it this way: this view was opposed in Iran by

24

many of the ayatollahs. One of them criticized the decision on a number of grounds. He said first that you have been deceived, because here you are passing judgement on a book you haven't read, you pass the sentence on a man you have not tried, and you are being drawn into conflict which is neither necessary nor profitable. That was the gist of the statement of Ayatollah Muntazari, who was designated successor to Ayatollah Khomeini, and whom Ayatollah Khomeini described as the apple of his eye, the fruit of his labour as a scholar. So you can see that the views of Ayatollah Khomeini were not agreed to unanimously, even by the scholars of Islam.'

The differences between Sunni and Shia Muslims are by no means negligible, however much each group may recognize the other as Muslim.

'I think there is conflict. I think historically it's been as great as that between Catholics and Protestants in Northern Ireland. It isn't really so much because the liturgy is so different, or because the way that they practise their Faith is different, but really because of ingrained hostilities and suspicions between the communities. The Shia, as I think it's commonly said, have always been the underdogs, and there's been a lot of secrecy, because they have felt threatened by the sea of Sunni Muslims surrounding them. If one was to study the Islamic law, there's not that many differences between them, and I think it's possible to accept them in the same way that we accept the other four Sunni schools of law. That's my view.'

But although these different communities have the theoretical means to recognize each other, in practice the division can be violent and extreme. While the World Service programmes were being made, four men claiming to represent Hizb'ullah (the 'Party of God', a pro-Iranian Shia movement) called a press conference 'to vow revenge against Saudi Arabia

25

and Kuwait for the beheading of sixteen Shia Muslims accused of causing bomb explosions in Mecca last July'. The holy places of pilgrimage in and around Mecca and Medina are in Saudi Arabia (which is predominantly Sunni), and to some Muslims the rulers of that country are not worthy guardians of the cradle of Islam. Or again, to come down to the present, violence between the communities, of a savage kind, broke out in Karachi in 1995.

So we started with a simple and God-commanded vision of community, of umma, of a single family of the faithful living as the servants of God in the world of His creation. But we have begun to see the possibility of deep conflict which has clear and extensive political consequences.

Such conflict cannot be resolved within the majority community, the Sunnis, by an appeal to one, supreme authority, because there is no human authority of that kind. Once there was a single, recognized Caliph but even he was subject to advice – not least because Sharia is itself open to continuing debate and interpretation.

Decrees and Interpretations

The main ways of interpretation are *qiyas* (analogy from the established to the unknown or novel circumstance) and *ijma'* (consensus in the community); *ijtihad* (a particular effort at interpretation on the part of those qualified to do so) is thought by some to have been restricted to the early centuries, though in practice it continues. But even if an interpretation issues in a *fatwa* or decree, it is not necessarily binding on all Muslims:

'A fatwa is an Islamic decree that interprets the existing instructions which are available, both in the Qur'ān and in the Sunna – that is, the prophetic tradition. It can never overrule the Qur'ān or the prophetic tradition.'

JB: 'Who can issue a fatwa, and what authority does a fatwa have for Muslims in the world?'

'We ought to state here very clearly that Islam does not know any institutionalized priesthood. Islam has no system of clergymen. Those learned enough in the Qur'ān and the prophetic tradition, either by memorizing them or by knowing exactly where to find whatever is relevant, may be competent enough to take decisions relating to themselves or to a limited number of other people. If they have not got the competence, they should abstain from issuing any such statements; but if they feel that they have the competence, they are entitled to do so without needing the approval of anybody. However, they need to bring proof for their statements; they need to substantiate their statements with proof from the Qur'ān and the Sunna. And this proof may again be challenged by anybody. When the Caliph Umar stated that a limit should be put on the amount of dowry that may rightfully be given to a bride, he was challenged by an old lady, and he accepted the challenge, because she quoted an *aya*, a verse of the Qur'ān. He did not say, "Well, I am the Caliph and I am in power, I have more knowledge and I spent time myself with the Prophet, and who are you to challenge me?" So if a fatwa does not stand on good ground, if it does not have good footing, then there is no obligation on any Muslim to follow it, because it is based on an interpretation of the law; and if it sets out from false premisses, then it cannot stand. Every single Muslim is responsible to God for his deeds, and nobody can take that burden off his shoulders. However, we also have the statement of the Prophet, "My people can never agree in error". So if the learned people of the nation or the people altogether agree on something, then we have an indication that this certain fatwa, this decree, stands.'

The ulama are thus of the greatest possible importance in

this process of debate and decision:

'Ulama is the plural of *'alim;* they are those who are learned. Usually this term is used for those who are learned in matters of religion, but of course you can be a learned person in technical matters, or in many other areas of life. You would then be an alim in this particular field. But relating to religious knowledge (that is, *fiqh,* Islamic jurisprudence), the ulama are those who have acquired sufficient knowledge to form their own independent judgement on issues relating to the area that they have studied. So anybody can become an alim, who acquires that knowledge and competence.'

It follows that there is in Islam no final, Vatican-like, authority:

'We don't have a Vatican, we do not have a Pope. No one can give me a fatwa in Mecca or Riyadh or Tehran or Cairo and tell me that I've got to follow it. I, an individual scholar, can challenge anyone. And I do, very often. And I stand my ground, I argue my case, and I challenge them to argue against it. So my vision of the Muslim community here [in the UK] is that it should have its own scholars. That is why we have established the Muslim College in this country: we will have our own scholars, home-grown, familiar with our problems, and then they will deal with everything in consultation, as the ideal Muslim society should be.'

Once again, we return to the emphatic stress on the individual accountability and responsibility of each Muslim, and this is no light matter. On the Day of Judgement, to which Muslims believe that all humans are heading, each individual will be responsible for his or her own actions. There can be no appeal to the authority of others who may have commanded him or her to do wrong. Each person's acts will be weighed exactly:

'Somewhere in the Qur'ān it says that the genuineness of a

Muslim's belief is between himself and God. Ultimately we are not there to make the judgement. It is up to the Divine Power to decide, hence the Day of Judgement, and the great implication of the Day of Judgement is that you are responsible for your conscience and faith. You are not to look all the time over your shoulder to some power-structure which tries to impose its values on you.'

JB: 'Do you believe that you yourself are going to be standing in some particular place in the future, on an actual Day of Judgement?'

'When the trumpet sounds? I don't know. I don't know. And somewhere inside me, it's not my business. My business is actually to live my life *now*, and to live it in a way that is creative, responsive, and to throw out energy which we can call love and compassion.'

That in itself is an individual interpretation of the relation of our life now to the final judgement of it. And it brings us back to the central paradox of Islam. Islam is indeed open to diverse interpretation, so that there is no single voice of Islam. It depends for its own health and style on debate and discussion, and it can assume very different cultural forms in different parts of the world. Within the UK the Muslim community is an anthology of different styles and allegiances which reflect the original countries of origin of the immigrants, and also, in some cases, the continuing connections with other Muslim countries. Yet at the same time it is clearly possible to identify Muslims as Muslims in terms of what they hold in common. That is because the foundations of Islam are extremely simple and not in the least open to negotiation or change. What may be happening – helping to create the impression for outsiders that the whole of Islam is dictatorial and non-negotiable – is that some groups may be extending the boundary of the non-negotiable far out, into domains where absolute conformity is neither desirable nor Islamic.

The Five Pillars

The non-negotiable foundations of Islam are actually extremely simple and practical. They are non-negotiable because they are established in the Qur'ān, and they can be summarized as the seven articles of *iman*, or faith, and the five pillars. On these, all Muslims agree:

The five pillars are meant to perform important functions for the Muslim – they are meant to perform the process of purification, and to fill a vacuum with the ethics of Islam, which is our development. As a result, the five important pillars of Islam are: first, the *ash-shahada*, which means witness, and this witness must result in action, of which the first process must be prayer. So the second pillar is prayer, and that means prayer during the periods of the day, as well as on special occasions during the year. In Islam, prayer has a wider significance, in the sense that it is meant to help the individual, or to help me as a person, to develop my consciousness of the Creator – God, or Allah in Arabic. The third important pillar is that of fasting so that I am able to come to terms with what it must be like for those who have to go without food for most of their lives, for one reason or another. I therefore develop an understanding, a sympathy, an empathy with that particular condition. The fourth pillar would therefore result in my contributing financially to the needs of people who are suffering in the world. This is done through the *zakat*, where I have to contribute 2.5% of my savings to the needy and disadvantaged in the Muslim community, and if the Muslim community has been taken care of, then beyond the Muslim community to non-Muslims. Those important pillars set me on the road of sacrifice, perseverance and patience. These kinds of virtues are encapsulated for me in the fifth pillar, the *hajj*, or pilgrimage to Mecca, where the *hajj* becomes the ultimate sacrifice, which I am prepared to make. It is a pilgrimage, not only to Mecca, but a pilgrimage also towards my Creator, towards God, so that I can reflect the attributes of God, the attributes of mercy, compassion, love, of concern for others, of repentance, forgiveness. I have to reflect these in my own life, in my interaction with my fellow human beings, and also in relation to the rest of creation.'

Iman, or faith, is already contained in the first of the five pillars, *ash-shahada*, the witness:

'This witness is articulated by the individual Muslim, or by myself for instance, by saying *La ilaha illa'Llahu wa-Muhammad rasulu'Llah*. This means, "There is no God but one God, and Muhammad is the messenger of God." This is a statement of intent for me, but in Islam this is not enough. There must be a movement from a statement of intent to an action or reflection of that intent in everyday life. As a result, I must fulfil the four further pillars to make me an active Muslim. The fulfilment of that Shahada should result in peace out of the concern for justice, and for all human beings and for the environment in which I live.'

The Seven Articles of Faith

But the seven basic articles of faith can nevertheless be distinguished from the pillars:

'They are, first of all: the unity of the Godhead; secondly, belief in the angels; third, belief in the Books, in all the revealed Books, up to the Qur'ān; fourthly, belief in the prophets, from Adam up to the Prophet Muhammad (peace be on all of them);

31

then fifth, in Doomsday; then sixth in what is called *qadr*, that is, on destiny determined by God, with happiness and misery both coming from God; and the seventh is life after death.'

It follows from the foundational importance of the five pillars that Islam is a way of life (in Arabic *din*) rather than a religion, if by religion is meant something that might be added on to life by way of a particular set of beliefs:

'Islam is a way of life, not just a religion. Unfortunately it has always been understood as merely a religion in the Christian sense – or in the secular sense rather, that religion and other affairs have nothing to do with each other. Islam penetrates all areas of life. For Muslims it is *the* way of life. For anybody else it would be a way of life, for us it is the only way of life, as regards ourselves; and as the way of life, Islam guides Muslims, not just in matters of worship, but in daily matters as well. For Muslims, anything they do where they do not forget Allah, and where they intend good, is an act of worship – whether it's helping your neighbour or whether it's operating a machine that you work on or driving a car – it is an act of worship if it is done with the right intention. Muslims believe that intentions are the key to success. People cannot always be judged by the outcome of their work. What is important is that they do whatever they do with good intention. So as a way of life, Muslims feel that they have a right to enter into discussion of issues which are not *per se* religious. From an Islamic point of view, they feel that they are qualified to talk about economics, about education, about home affairs, about defence matters, about politics, about social affairs, about things that concern people as they live together. What we endeavour to achieve is a harmonious society where people have the right to abide by their principles, by their set of values.'

32

The Permitted and the Forbidden

For Muslims, their way of life (the Sunna) is extremely detailed, however simple the general principles are. Sharia defines very explicitly what, in human behaviour, is *haram* (forbidden) and *halal* (permitted) – and what is *halal* applies to very much more than the way animals are slaughtered for meat, though that is the most familiar occurrence of the word, creating, as it does, anxiety for those concerned for animal welfare. Muslims reply that the detailed prescriptions are more compassionate; but in any case (since the animals involved can scarcely be consulted), the conditions of what is *halal* cannot be negotiated, because they come from God. The detailed prescriptions for *haram* and *halal* apply just as much to all aspects of life, and issue, for example, in careful rules of washing and cleanliness. These are important to Muslims as a kind of 'check-list' – a practical way in which they can know for sure whether their life is being offered in *islam* to God:

'I think these detailed rules are important. I think that faith is as faith does. This is not to say that most Muslims do not fail by these extremely difficult standards: these are a part of the failings of our common humanity. But there is an important need for people to recognize these lapses as an occasion for self-criticism. If they do not, then it is very questionable whether they are believers.'

JB: 'But why should a prohibition on eating pork or drinking alcohol be singled out as a language of self-criticism?'

'All the dietary laws relate to issues of human harm and good, and alcohol is an obvious instance of that. They relate to what is a wholesome way of living one's life. In the area of sexuality and its relationship to law, this is even more obvious, to know what would be a proper enjoyment of the sexual appetite as opposed to a prostitution of it. So Islam has a complete underlying attitude here, that whatever is within the limit set by God should be enjoyed with a wholesome appetite, and whatever is forbidden (and there are always reasons why that is forbidden) should be avoided as far as is humanly possible. Beyond that, of course, God is merciful – there will always be failings and lapses. But what is crucial is that these failings must be seen as an occasion for self-criticism. If they are not, then, as I said, the faith of that individual is quite insecure. Possibly he is a liar, in fact, or a hypocrite, or weak-willed maybe.'

So the issue for Muslims is not one of conformity but of conscience. It is a matter of what one is going to present as the consequence of one's life on the Day of Judgement:

'Islam offers two rewards: this life itself is so full, it's so rewarding, it's so perfect, and that's the first reward. But then secondly there is the reward to be given on the Day of Judgement, and that is Paradise and all the wonderful things that are described in Paradise in the Qur'ān. That's the second reward: it's reward upon reward, if you live the way that your own nature demands. You see, Islam is not asking you to be someone else to get that reward. It is asking you to be yourself, to be a human being and not an animal – to live like a human being and not to live like a dog in the street.'

Fundamentals, Fundamentalism and Interpretation

All this means that although there are non-negotiable fundamentals in Islam, which lie at the root of all Muslim life, Muslims cannot wisely or helpfully be described as fundamentalists, because their creative and lived relation to revelation is not of that kind:

'There is nothing called fundamentalism in Islam, because

this is a Western concept. So far as Muslims are concerned Islam is such a complete way of life, and the Prophet's instances and examples are so much there in front of us, and there is so much scope for variation, that if anyone says, this is the *only* way to be Muslim, then this is wrong. There are certain things of course – for example, those five pillars, those basic things – which cannot really change.'

JB: 'But the impression to the outsider is that Muslims are prepared to fight and kill others to defend those basic things.'

'That fighting is a different matter. If you look at the fighting and at what is happening in various countries, all that is very different from our discussion about the essence of Islam. If we talk about practising Islam, then you can say, is there any Muslim country which is practising Islam properly? There is not a single Muslim country which is truly and entirely Islamic. Take Bangladesh, Malaysia, Indonesia, even Saudi Arabia – even there not all the laws are entirely Islamic; there are certain criminal laws, but they could not implement all the civil laws (for example, it is not an entirely interest-free economy). So how can we say that there is a single country which is truly Islamic, in the same sense that Medina was Islamic, for example, during the days of the Prophet or of the early Caliphate? It's not there. So it would be wrong on our part, or on anybody's part, to assume that this fighting is Islamic fundamentalism. You may call it fundamentalism, or any "ism" you like, but this kind of fighting that is going on – among the Muslims in Beirut for example – is that Islamic? I do not consider it Islamic, any more than I consider what the Jews are doing to the Muslims is really religious from the Judaic point of view.'

JB: 'The "ism" that many mention is "fanaticism".'

'That is another Western word. If you take the dictionary meaning as one who does not use reason but is guided only by emotions and feelings, and takes a particular point of view and becomes aggressive about it, that cannot possibly be Islamic and I do not support it.'

The point to be grasped is that the roots of Islam, exhibited in common and relatively simple behaviours, are secure and deep, but that the tree of lived interpretation continues to grow. For that growth to happen, dissent, discussion and argument are essential:

'Let me explain this because it is very important – and it is a point often missed by many jurists even within the Muslim community. We have three aspects of our system: first, belief; second, worship; third, human relations, or the laws that control human relations. In matters of belief, in matters of worship, we rely on the revelation. Our human efforts of interpretation there are limited. They have to be limited, because we rely on what God has told us through the Prophet: that there is one God. We are not going to argue about this, or discuss it, or find reasons for it: we accept it. We believe in the one God – that there is a Day of Judgement. The acts of worship, the manner in which we pray or fast or give alms or perform the pilgrimage, this is all prescribed. We do not argue about it. We neither subtract from it, nor add to it. So this is the area outside human endeavour. Anything else, within the area of human relations, is subject to the human condition, and therefore the jurists have enormous authority there.

'Now, to give an example, scientists are telling us that the earth cannot sustain more than so many people, and therefore we have to sit down round the table and decide on the level of human population on this planet. Muslims can take part in this and can participate meaningfully – providing of course that they are not being asked to reduce their number as the only ones to pay the penalty for the earth's pollution. But otherwise, on such matters, Muslims are free to argue and participate in discussion. Now unfortunately, there are many Muslim scholars who do not differentiate between these three spheres, and therefore they find themselves bound by decisions or ideas of earlier scholars, and they call *that* the Sharia, which is there and we have to obey it as it is in the books. But those books are not books of revelation. They are books of human endeavour, which we are not only allowed to question, but are asked to question, and to try to develop what is there. Without developing it, Islam would become moribund, completely irrelevant to the modern situation.'

JB: 'But that is exactly what some outsiders think it is.'

'The reality is that the Muslims *are* changing. In practice they are. You might hear a lot of shouting, of people being pulled by the scruff of their necks into the modern world, shouting loudly against it while they are living in it. But really the shouting does not constitute the true expression of Islam. It *is* a real protest. But let me put it this way: many communities, when they lose certain aspects of their culture, mourn it. They feel like someone losing a child. But shouting and mourning for a child doesn't mean that the child is coming back. You have to accept the death of the child. There are certain aspects of our culture which *have* to go, but these are aspects not to do with the fundamental beliefs, nor to do with the fundamental acts of worship, which remain in place. We may perceive our relationship with God differently, because of our development in our knowledge of science and technology and what have you, but that does not in any way impinge on our belief in the one God. He remains there.'

JB: 'Which aspects have to go?'

'This is to do with the social system. Most of the Sharia laws were written under the Abbasids, and towards the end of the Umayyads, so they are a reflection of the society of the time. And these aspects have to go – for instance, the treatment of women. We will most certainly change our attitude to women, and our idea of social organization, of human relations, will certainly change.'

The Recovery of Islam

Here is a large programme, of which Muslims should not be afraid. Indeed, as we shall see, Muslims should themselves be giving a lead to the world at large, as they once did. But all the Muslims we listened to in these programmes were agreed that that is not the reality of the Muslim world at the present time: 'Can one find a single practising Islamic state in the world?' Everyone gave the same answer – no. There are, of course, good reasons for this: the dramatic turmoils of the last hundred years have seen the end of the single Caliphate at the cessation of the Ottoman empire, the end of colonialism, the rise of the superpowers and the deprivations of the Third World. There have been immense local pressures on Muslim communities in countries where they have settled, such as the United Kingdom; and at points of strain, any string may snap:

'If you look at the Muslim community here in Britain, for the last thirty to forty years, although we have come from different parts of the world, we have worked very hard, we have worked unsocial hours, sometimes we have worked in the places where nobody else wanted to work. If you look at the health services, the transport system, the small corner shops, the Muslim community is doing its best to contribute to the economy, and to work hard to earn a living. You have not seen so far any complimentary remarks about the Muslim community or about the help they are giving or about the way they are contributing to society. But you get some minute thing – say, some disturbance at a football match – and they get reported as Muslims. I think it must be clear that we are human beings and that we will have our shortfalls, but if you compare our record with other communities, I must say that in many cases it will be better. But in any society, when a minority which is part and parcel of that society does not get fair treatment, then it starts looking for support outside, or for different ways. The Muslim community lives here, we work here, we want to be part of society; all we want is to practise our own religion without fear, offensive words and condemnation.

'Now a good society is judged by the way they treat their minorities, but if we take one example here, the figures which were published in Bradford three years ago: only thirty-three per cent of all the school leavers were successful in getting jobs within one year of leaving school, and thirty-three per cent is a very low figure, but if you look at the figure for the Muslims, it is only 5.9% who were successful in getting jobs. So many of them think they should go after higher education, but even after higher qualification, if they still don't get a job, they are going to feel that much let down. We don't have any access to power, we will never be a majority community in this country, we will always be a minority and we will be dependent upon the good people in the majority who will give us our rights.'

So the local pressures on Muslims may be precisely the reason why their own practice of Islam becomes eroded, or why it is the case – as all the Muslims we listened to emphasized – that there is not yet a single Islamic state, as opposed to a state in which Muslims are a majority, anywhere in the world. What is the remedy? In part of course it is to remove the political and social impediments. But equally, the answer to this failure, for many Muslims, lies within the collective action of Islam itself.

The answer for them is to go, not forward into accommodation and compromise with the modern world, but back to Sharia. Sharia is the charter for human life and worth and behaviour which comes from God. The way forward for Islam is the way back:

'There are, in the world, countries which are Muslim states only because the vast majority of the people happen to be Muslims, and that is why they are called Muslim states. But they are distinct from an Islamic state where there is a conscious effort to realize the Sharia. I believe that many of the problems being faced by Muslims in Muslim countries, and by minority groups, arise because the Sharia is not in operation. Sharia would both protect individual Muslims and provide them with their rights against a powerful state, and it would protect the rights of any minority against a large community of Muslims, as well as the state itself. All those rights can be better realized within the framework of Sharia. This practical quest for Sharia is not new. From the very beginning of Islam, from the time when the Prophet was in Medina, the first thing he did after establishing the *masjid* [mosque] was to create a constitution, known as the Constitution of Medina, whereby not only the new Muslim community, but also the Zoroastrians, the Christians and the Jews, as well as non-religious people, could co-operate together, to meet the needs of the city state. That to me is a model of how an Islamic state is going to meet the needs of all its citizens.'

'Muslims should go back to the Qur'ān and Sunna. That's how they can recover. They are not following the basic principles and they must go back to these. Of course to do that is very difficult, because the whole world has become charged with the system which has developed in the West, which is not religious, which is not even Christian. Therefore I would ask the entire world to go back to the religious tradition.'

'Our role today is not to keep going forward into more and more adaptations, but to keep going back – back to the beginning to see what the Qur'ān and the Hadith say. If (and it's a very big "if", because usually the answer is there) it is not clear, then we move to the early scholars, because they are the best. It is the early generation who are the best people who were ever created, the best people who practised Islam in its most perfect form.'

JB: 'But the Qur'ān is related to particular circumstances; it was revealed in relation to an age and a world which are not our own. So if, to take an example, we are talking about what a Muslim should do by way of recreation, archery and hunting are recommended as very good. But that is hardly relevant to living in Bradford.'

'The reasons for that are that the Muslims were continually at war, and so the Prophet said that it is very important for Muslims to build up their capacity as soldiers. So therefore today, if we don't learn archery, Muslim children should be taught how to shoot, because the arrow has been replaced by the gun. This system of analogy is extremely important. Once you have the system of analogy, everything is extremely simple.'

But those answers also summarize exactly the fears which were expressed by non-Muslims at the outset. Muslims claim (and we shall see more of this in detail) that the return to Sharia would create an exemplary society, and one in which all people, Muslims and non-Muslims alike, would be glad to live. But the outsider has the impression that the laws in Sharia contain fierce attitudes to those who are not Muslim, savage punishments for the sexually aberrant, paternalistic subordination of women, and intolerant policies for education.

Is that *really* so? What do Muslims *actually* believe about such things? What *would* Sharia mean if it were recovered for life and law in this or any other country? These are the questions to which we can now turn.

CHAPTER TWO

THE INTERPRETATION OF THE QUR'ĀN AND ISSUES OF
JUDGEMENT: INTEREST, THEFT, ADULTERY AND
HOMOSEXUALITY

Interpretations of the Qur'ān

Islam is a religion (though some have said it is not a religion but
a way of life) which rests on the Qur'ān as the revealed, absolute
and uncompromised Word of God. But the Qur'ān was revealed
through Muhammad in the sixth century of the Christian era, in
Arabia, and it makes reference to people and events of that time,
hence also to the intellectual and social circumstances of that
time. Does this mean that Muslim life, based on the Qur'ān, is
'frozen' in the sixth century, and that it consists in reproducing
sixth-century life and attitudes in the twentieth or any other
century?

Certainly the Qur'ān *is* absolute and non-negotiable. But it
did not envisage or legislate for all future circumstances. From
the start, it was recognized that it had to be interpreted.

'The Qur'ān's authority is absolute. We look on the Qur'ān
as the Word of God. But we interpret the Qur'ān. And this
interpretation can be dynamic, and can change with the
circumstances. Let me take a particular example, what is known
as *riba* [receiving interest on money]: *riba* is clearly defined in the
Qur'ān so that any excess on capital is *riba*. If I lend you money

and demand anything in excess of my capital, then this is *riba*, and this is prohibited. This is regarded as one of the greatest sins in Islam, to make profit out of a loan. Now the issue here of interpretation is this: no Muslim will ever say that *riba* is permissible, no Muslim scholar would dare say so. The question and the dispute will arise over the definition of *riba*, whether the definition includes bank interest or does not; whether it includes certain economic activities or it does not. So you find that, while agreeing with the basic text, it becomes a matter of categorizing what comes under that particular term *riba*. So according to the information that I have, the Mufti in Egypt is about to issue a fatwa to say that there is no real lending on the part of the depositor, nor borrowing on the part of the bank. It is really an investment, in which the depositor says, "Use this on my behalf." The bank does not need the money, so there is no way you can say that this is similar to an individual who needs to buy food and says, "Lend me £100 to buy food and I'll pay you £110 at the end of the month." That's a totally different situation. Therefore you cannot call the profit or interest accrued to the investor or depositor *riba*.

'So you find that the Qur'ān will remain always sacred: no change in it at all. But you will look upon a situation and a definition differently. Let me cite another example: in one situation in particular the second Caliph of Islam, Umar, actually changed certain rules in the Qur'ān, quite openly. He said that the circumstances had now changed. This was in reference to a payment from the *zakat* fund, the collective tax that we pay, to people who were on the edge of becoming Muslim. They were given payment in recognition of their alliance to Islam, to sweeten them, so to speak, to bring them to Islam. They are called "the people whose hearts you want to win over". Now these people were paid by the Prophet, they were paid by the

44

first Caliph, but when the second Caliph came, he suspended the payment. When they came to demand it, he said, "Look, Islam is now strong, it does not need your support, and therefore we are not going to pay you." In other words, the Muslim scholars can look behind the edict of the Qur'ān, see the reason for it, and then interpret or pass legislation to meet the actual aim of the words as they are specified there.'

The Qur'ān, therefore, is limitless in meaning (there is no circumstance to which it cannot apply), but at the same time it has many levels of interpretation:

'The Qur'ān is such a deep fountain of knowledge that every day, every time I read it, I discover something for the first time – it's so profound, it's so beautiful, there's so much in there. That is the great miracle of the Qur'ān; that's what draws people so powerfully to Islam. People are converted through the Qur'ān because it's such a wonderful thing, the Word of God.'

But like any writing situated in a particular circumstance in time, it requires a bridge to be built from 'then' to 'now':

'If you have a text, a page of any writing, a letter sent from a friend to a friend, the letter is the same; what the person meant in his letter is also the same, but if you get two people to read the same letter, you will get two different conclusions, simply because they are of different levels of intelligence. They have different backgrounds. People see things through their own culture. So the differences in interpretation are due to differences in levels of intelligence, differences in background, differences in culture, differences in experience. This does not affect the fact that what God meant is what God meant. But one of the great things about the Qur'ān is that it has different levels of the very same verse. You have different levels of understanding. The more intelligent you are the more you grasp.'

JB: 'Does that mean that a person of the highest

intelligence and training can attain to "what God meant"?'

'Indeed. What God meant is like a river. You go to the river to get some water. There is one person who has a thimble in his hand, and he can only fill that much. There is another who has a cup, and he can fill a cupful of water. And there is another who gets a bucket, and he gets more. It depends on how big your container is as to how much you get out of the river.'

JB: 'But does that mean that a person of lower intelligence is in some sense defective in understanding the Qur'ān? And if understanding is dependent on intelligence, why, after centuries of highly intelligent study of the Qur'ān, has the true meaning (what God meant to convey by it) not been established?'

'Many of the meanings of the Qur'ān *are* well discerned and worked out. Many of the meanings are known to the majority of the people. The point is that there can still be wrong interpretations. And when you touch on the less intelligent, and what they can get out of it, you find that they get a lot of it by their heart. They can feel the warmth of the language more than the very intelligent. One of the beauties of the style and language of the Qur'ān is that it speaks to the heart as well as to the mind, and as strongly to the heart as to the mind.'

JB: 'Can you give me any examples of a wrong interpretation that has to be corrected?'

'Yes, I can give you an example which caused a lot of bloodshed, in the early days of Islam. There is a verse [of the Qur'ān] which says that it is to God that judgement belongs. And of course you and I would agree: He is the king, so of course judgement belongs to Him. But in the early history a group emerged who took it to mean that no person has the right to judge between two people, and that anyone who does so is blasphemous. That is a stupid interpretation because the same Qur'ān gives instruction on how such judgement should be carried out – as for instance, when a man has a matrimonial difference with his wife, the Qur'ān instructs that a judge from her side and a judge from his should come between the two to mend things. What God meant in the other verse is the judgement in the Day of Judgement. Yet there was a lot of bloodshed caused by this misinterpretation, and blood shed by some of the most pious people in Islam.'

JB: 'Are there examples of misinterpretation in the contemporary world, which might equally lead to bloodshed?'

'History, I am afraid, does repeat itself quite often. There has been a fringe lunatic group recently which has judged that it is unlawful, from the Islamic point of view, to live in a society in which there are many people who are sinful. What rubbish! God doesn't send prophets to the people who are righteous, He sends them to the people who are sinners, to teach them and guide them. But the way to deal with this is to expose the triviality, and stupidity of the interpretation, and in the end treat it more tolerantly.'

So to describe Muslims in general as 'fundamentalist' in relation to the Qur'ān is extremely misleading because it conceals the issue of exegesis which Muslims themselves recognize. They are perfectly well aware that language can be symbolic and metaphorical, as well as literal and descriptive:

'There is a verse in the Qur'ān which points out that there are many allegorical verses in the Qur'ān, and there is much meaning which is allegorical. There are many different levels of interpretation, and I think that people will seek out and accept what is suitable for their particular needs at the time.'

'The Qur'ān is written in language. Unfortunately – or perhaps fortunately – language is not transparent. Language is open to interpretation. Indeed, in the Islamic tradition, we talk about a multitude of levels of meaning – hence exegesis, hence commentary; and commentaries sometimes conflict with one another on the surface. The Qur'ān needs to be read with tremendous insight and wisdom, and with the ability to interpret. Let's take the parallel of music: there are lots of technically able pianists today, of great brilliance. But their interpretations are different, coming from whole cultural understandings, which are part of their blood, and it comes through in the playing.'

JB: 'Auden once observed that every high C accurately struck demolished the theory that we are the irresponsible puppets of fate or chance. Are you saying that the Qur'ān will reach us on many different levels, but that one is closer to the aesthetic reach of music – not necessarily saying something by way of literal description, but moving us by its own quality in the direction of hope?'

'For me personally that's absolutely right. That's why I chose the example of music. Indeed, the Qur'ān – ironically – is music. I say "ironically", because there are a lot of Muslims who fulminate against music and say that they're not sure it's a good thing at all. But the fact is that the Qur'ān is music.'

JB: 'Can language ever be literal?'

'On a very simplistic basis, yes, on the level of giving you directions to go to the Gents, or whatever, directions of that kind. But for me language is always multi-layered and ambiguous, always ambiguous. There are many literary theorists who talk of the lack of necessity for having an author; the text lives its own life, or rather, the text is there and only comes to life when the reader reads the text. The intention of the author becomes very secondary. If we accept that the text of the Qur'ān is the Word of God, God is infinite, His mind is infinite, but we are finite. We can only get little chips of that understanding, and the levels of understanding that we reach depend on our own spiritual station. There is a paradox here: Islam is an egalitarian religion, which has preached social justice historically, and yet there is also a hierarchy of spiritual growth. So the idea of symbols and metaphor is not foreign to Islam. In fact, it is one of the fundamentals of Islam in the classical sense that the world is a symbol, and the universe is a symbol, and everything in the universe has symbolic merit. It is not just Sūfīsm [an extensive mystical movement and practice in Islam] which lends itself to images and music and art.'

Of course there have to be controls over all possible interpretations: not all interpretations become true simply by being called symbolic:

'I think it's really sad when people do that and give a symbolic interpretation of the Qur'ān, because then they can come up with any kind of interpretation and say it's symbolic. The Qur'ān is very clear, the Hadiths of the Prophet are very clear.'

The Sūfī interpretation means that even stories in the Qur'ān which appear to be straightforward descriptions have a symbolic meaning. Thus the Qur'ān tells of the origin of the human race in the creation of Adam and Eve (and we will see later how Muslims evaluate the relation of that story to theories of evolution):

'The Sūfī and other philosophers of the Middle Ages treated almost all the stories in the Qur'ān – and all the holy books in the tradition, and Christianity as well – as being symbolic. They are not real persons or situations, but represent the relations between man and God. Therefore Adam becomes the human race, and the whole drama is to describe the relationship between man and God.'

JB: 'Is that still a legitimate way to interpret the Qur'ān today?'

'The word "legitimate" is a difficult thing for us, because the word "legitimate" means that we have an authority to legitimize things. But we don't. We have no Vatican. So anyone can put his view, as long as he can put forward the evidence and cogent argument; such views would be respected. It doesn't mean that everyone else will accept them or follow them. But they are still within the boundaries of Islam.'

JB: 'Let me take another example: the Qur'ān describes in very literal terms both heaven and hell. If we send a spacecraft to look, will we find them as literal places in the universe somewhere?'

'No, I don't think so. This is really one of the things, the Fire and the Garden, which are in the knowledge of God. We do not know where they are. I cannot send a letter addressed to Paradise, just left of Uranus, or whatever. Not only that, but there was a tremendous argument among the scholars of the time that heaven and hell are not in existence now, they will be created later. We certainly cannot find them now.'

Interpretations of Sharia

So the Qur'ān is open to interpretation in many different ways. The first interpreters were Muhammad and his companions, because they were in effect living commentaries on the Qur'ān. That is why Hadith has authority in Islam. The different schools of Sharia are derived, ultimately, from the combination of the Qur'ān and Hadith, and form the organized patterns of life, themselves varied, in which Muslims live.

Sharia is very much more detailed than the Qur'ān in specifying what is *halal* and *haram* in everyday life, and in providing legislation. It is in Hadith and Sharia that some of the items so familiar to the non-Muslim are specified: the punishment for theft and adultery, the treatment of apostates, the prohibition on *riba* [interest]. It is because Sharia represents the collective efforts of Muslims to create ordered expressions of the life which God wills and intends in the Qur'ān that the assertion was made so strongly, at the end of the last chapter, that the way forward for Islam is the way back to Sharia.

Does this mean that Muslim life is frozen, if not in the sixth century of the Christian era, then in something like the eighth or ninth, when the schools of Sharia were being formed? Are Muslims fundamentalist, if not in relation to the Qur'ān, then certainly in relation to Sharia?

In fact, not so. Sharia itself is open to interpretation and extension, and indeed demands it:

'The Qur'ān and the Sunna have to be interpreted as society progresses, or as time goes by. Everything has to be interpreted. What often happens with the schools of the law is that a person, because of lack of knowledge, does not know all the Hadiths, for example; the Qur'ān is there before us, but the Hadiths are scattered. And we have seen, without any disrespect for the founders of the law schools, that they've made mistakes, because they are human beings.'

The community itself has recognized procedures for seeking the true and continuing interpretations. The best known are *ijma'*, *qiyas* and *ijtihad*:

'Issues like artificial insemination or genetic engineering are new issues which the ulama, the scholars of Sharia, will have to investigate, and are doing so. That is why there is a whole movement in the Muslim world which can be put under the umbrella of the movement of "Islamization". This is a movement at a very high intellectual level, where Muslims are examining contemporary issues, no matter what they may be, whether in the pure sciences or in the arts, and they are trying to examine them with the backcloth of the Sharia. They are having to examine the roots of knowledge in the West and the roots of knowledge in Islamic civilization, and see where they meet. All these new issues have to be investigated. The Sharia is a dynamic framework. It has to meet new situations and new times facing it.'

Banking and Interest

An example of this process would be the exploration of how the Islamic banking system can operate in the contemporary world without compromising such things as the prohibition on *riba*:

'The basic thing about the Islamic economic system is that it is continuously evolving. You are bound by what is prohibited as opposed to the structures. That is why, for instance, in Iran there is a tremendous and heated debate going on about whether the state should be interventionist or whether there should be a mixed economy with a bit of nationalization and a bit of free enterprise. This is a part of the evolving process in the spirit of *ijtihad*.'

What, then, would it actually mean to apply Sharia to these issues, which to the outsider create the impression of Islam fixed and frozen in the past? Is it, for example, realistic to think of the world economy being run without *riba*? We have already seen that *riba* is absolutely forbidden, and that is clearly non-negotiable, for all Muslims.

'On this the Qur'ān has made some very basic statements, about economics, in the sense that interest is discouraged greatly. It's seen as one of the major crimes. Allah and his Prophet, so the Qur'ān tells us, have declared war on interest. Now we have to look at why that is the case, and today, in an interest-based economy, we find that the majority of social suffering springs from the very fact that money is brought into

circulation bearing an interest charge. We have both inflation
and unemployment due to that fact. All this suffering would end
if there was a determination to put a stop to it by issuing money
in the first place that didn't bear an interest charge. A non-
interest economy can work and can succeed, and it can survive
on a much lower tax basis: you would have low tax and high
return instead of high tax and low return, because most of the tax
now serves to pay off the national debt.'

But within the overall context of that prohibition, there is
still room for interpretation of what counts as *riba*. We have
already heard of the possibility that a fatwa may be issued in
Egypt exempting bank deposits. I asked an expert in the Islamic
banking system for his reaction to that possibility:

'I have heard of this, but I don't think that kind of thinking
will catch on among the mainstream Islamic financial
institutions. They are very strict on that, and they believe that
once they allow that, other such concessions will follow, which
could undermine the Islamic banking system.'

JB: 'How, then, can any changes take place?'

'This has been a major problem within the Islamic banking
movement. You have various institutions with their own Sharia
advisory boards, and there have been contradictory and different
interpretations of the same issue – as, for example, the questions
of mark-up on a cost-plus financing operation, or even trading in
certain commodities. The Jedda-based Islamic Development
Bank, which is the pan-Islamic bank set up under the guidance of
the late King Faisal, has recently managed to get together a
number of ulama from various countries, and they have come up
with what they claim to be the master-plan for Islamic banking
laws and regulations, and they hope that, through the
International Association of Islamic Banks, this will be used and
recognized by all the Islamic financial institutions as the

authoritative body. But the differences remain, and I think they
have more to do with politics than with the interpretation of
Islamic law. As matters stand now, there are certain ulama who
say that, if you are living in a non-Muslim country, you are
justified to a certain extent in having interest-bearing accounts,
and once again, the whole concept of interest is in question.
Since you are not lending money for the gain of exorbitant
advantage in the use of that money, you can, if you are living in a
non-Muslim country, hold an account in a conventional bank
and receive interest. But I think it will still take some
considerable time to resolve this issue.'

What, then, are the basic boundaries set by the Qur'ān?

'There must be an element of risk-sharing in any financial
transaction, either on the profit side or on the loss side, and
there must be productive use of resources. The whole concept of
money is different in the Islamic financial system: money cannot
be traded as a commodity. Its value is basically fixed. You cannot
speculate in money, or in precious metals. The profit motive is
strong. Islam has nothing against making a profit, but it is against
the making of exorbitant profits or the misuse of profit and
wealth. Speculation is expressly forbidden. However, you can
own shares, as long as the companies in which you hold them do
not participate in what are considered unIslamic activities – like
owning casinos or abattoirs where pork is slaughtered, or
producing or selling alcohol – that kind of thing. Unit trusts are
also allowed, and there are moves to introduce an Islamic unit
trust in this country.'

Of course it is a question whether any company can be
found which does not somewhere in its network have
involvements in unIslamic activities. But again, the Islamic
emphasis is on doing the best one can, conscientiously, to avoid
such companies, not on creating absolute conditions with no

mistakes allowed. Even so, the question remains whether the Islamic banking system *can* coexist with the capitalist system and work:

'There are about sixty major Islamic institutions throughout the world, including China, in the north, where there are many Muslims; and I hear the latest ones are in New Zealand, Houston, and Pasadena in California. These financial institutions claim that they *are* working, although there are severe constraints in the banking laws of the non-Muslim country concerned: there are requirements, such as the reserve funds, which are essentially against the risk element of Islamic finance. Then there are also a number of Islamic trading and investment companies in the Gulf, and in countries like Turkey and Malaysia and North Africa, and they operate successfully on these principles. So it can work. And it would have major advantages. For example, inflation in an Islamic economy is almost non-existent because of the element of risk-sharing and the element of productive use of resources. But the problem of Islamic banking at the moment is that a lot of research needs to be done in Islamic banking theory. At the moment the emphasis is on trade finance and project finance through the four major instruments: the *murababa* [cost-plus financing], the *musharaqa* [equity participation], the *mudaraba* [joint ventures], and *ijjara* [leasing contract]; these are the four classical Islamic institutions. Some countries do complain that the emphasis is on trade finance, and on short-term trade finance, and very little on project finance and venture capital, and that is serious for developing Muslim countries. Also the Islamic banks lack a secondary financial capital market. There is no way, for instance, that they can trade certificates of deposit under Islamic banking principles.'

JB: 'What you are describing is a system that might theoretically work?'

'Certainly. There were recently two in-house International Monetary Fund papers on Islamic banking, and both concluded that maybe an Islamic financial system is better suited to absorbing the shocks of the present debt crisis than the high-interest policies in the West.'

JB: 'So, yes: theoretically it might – your word was "maybe" – work better. But how do you close this immense gap in the Islamic world between what ought theoretically to be put into practice and what is in fact happening?'

'This is the crux of the matter, as you suggest. There is this tremendous gap, and I don't see, in the near future, that the gap will be closed. The Islamic banking movement is still nascent in its modern phase – it's only fifteen years old. It faces tremendous opposition even in some Muslim countries, where the so-called Western education élites perceive it in a way as a primitive system – nothing to do with the twentieth century. On the other hand, if you consider that there is on one estimate forty billion dollars circulating within the Islamic banking system, and that they are growing in numbers and in confidence, the least you have to say is that the Islamic banking system is here to stay.'

Penalties for Theft and Adultery

So the application of Sharia to modern circumstances is allowed and some change is possible. But any fundamental change (such as the abolition of the prohibition on *riba* altogether) would clearly be impossible. Does the same pattern apply to other issues often asked about by the outsider, for example, to the traditional penalties of execution for adultery, and of amputation of a hand for theft? Many Muslims see these penalties (though with clear qualifications which belong to their proper understanding) as highly desirable, because they act as deterrents:

'I long for their revival! It's something that I long for, that we have a revival throughout the Muslim world, because it would help society. In any case, non-Muslims have nothing to worry about, because if a non-Muslim commits, for example, adultery, he is immediately handed over to his own people, so there would be a Christian judge sitting there or a Jewish judge sitting there. We don't judge non-Muslims by Islam. We judge them by their own religions.'

That last point is important. Muslim law only applies to Muslims. In a true Islamic state (and we have already heard that no such state actually exists at the present time), non-Muslims would be judged by their own law:

'All penalties in Islam must be understood within the broad context of what we call the Sharia. Within this framework, Islam is very much concerned with the ethics of relationships between human beings. But the Sharia is applicable only to Muslims. Within an Islamic state – and we must be very clear here that we are talking about an Islamic state – non-Muslims have provision to be judged by their own legal regulations. In the contemporary world good examples of this are in Pakistan and Iran. Both their constitutions have articles which give rights to non-Muslims to be subject to their own law, but within the broad framework of the Sharia. Therefore the penalties in Islam are restricted to Muslims, because, as I said earlier, the Shahada, being a statement of witness, results in responsibility, and that responsibility must be taken seriously. So the penalties, such as the cutting off of the hands of thieves, or the stoning to death for adultery, are penalties of deterrence. Actually, they are not penalties, they are meant to have a deterrent role within the society. That is why they are so harsh. But there is a whole process of procedure that the Sharia must enact before it can come to the judgement of a particular individual. If one follows that process, it minimizes the possibility of people being punished wrongly. It also minimizes the possibility of such deterrents having to be put into action.

'If I could give you an example: in a country like Bangladesh, which we all know is a very poor country where there are people who are starving, supposing someone there who is starving takes from someone's table a piece of bread, in this particular situation it would of course be very hard to cut someone's hand off, to put it crudely, because the Sharia demands that such an individual should have been taken care of by the state. According to Sharia a condition of being the state is that the needs of its citizens should be met. One of the needs is food, another is clothing, then transportation, health, education and so on. So in this particular instance it is extremely unlikely that the penalty would be applied, and if it was it would be an abuse against the Sharia, in my understanding of the way in which the Sharia should operate.'

Even more to the point, the penalties are nothing like so obvious or fundamental as implied by the casual observation that the penalty for adultery in the Qur'ān is death:

'Let me say about adultery, there is no mention in the Qur'ān of adultery being punishable by capital punishment. It is really in the Tradition. And although all the Muslim schools take the view that adultery is punishable by death (for both parties, incidentally, and not just the woman as most people think), there is a school of law, which is not commonly known, which says that since there is no mention of this punishment in the Qur'ān, therefore we reject it. And let me say that when the Libyan government, in about 1970 or 1971, commissioned an Egyptian scholar to formulate the law for them according to Islamic law (and that scholar, 'Alī Mansur, was a prominent member of the

Muslim Brotherhood, or in other words a fundamentalist according to the Western definition), he formulated for them the crime of adultery and the punishment for it according to Islamic law, and he gave them two alternatives: one to say that it is a capital offence, and the other that it is not – take your pick. It is not mandatory and it can be argued. But let me say that even if you do take it as mandatory, if you take Muslim law, you have to take it *in toto*, that is, the law of evidence as well as punishment. The law of evidence for the crime of adultery, or *zina*, as we call it, is such as to make it virtually impossible to prove. This can really be established only by confession. Otherwise you have to have four eyewitnesses – you know, four men seeing the act itself. That's why the penalty was not really very common in the Muslim world.'

Homosexuality

So even in an area where the Tradition is strong and where its interpretation in the schools is virtually unanimous, there is still room for debate and argument, and there is no central authority, like a Vatican, which can impose, or attempt to impose, a final solution which all must accept. Would the same be true of an issue in ethics, particularly where our understanding of an issue has been changed by reflection or research? To take an example: homosexual behaviours are clearly disapproved of by the Qur'ān: 'What! Of all creatures, do you approach males and leave the wives whom your Lord has created for you? You certainly are a people transgressing altogether' (xxvi. 165). But the Qur'ān, being absolute in its principles but related contingently to the circumstances of its time, clearly could not relate to much later observations of homosexual behaviours among other creatures; nor could it comment on a possible condition of homosexuality, as opposed to homosexual acts, because a conceptual category of that kind was not available. Supposing the indications of current research were confirmed, which indicate that in any (human) population, about five per cent have a genetically based preparedness to interact with people of the same sex (so that consequently homosexual acts are not simply the result of volition on the part of those who would, if they had more insight or were less sinful, be heterosexual), could the Muslim attitude change?

'That's a difficult one, because, as you know, homosexuality in the Qur'ān is regarded as something revolting. People are told to keep away from it. It is unnatural, it is wrong, it is something disgusting. Basically, Muslims would have to reconcile themselves to it, if it is true that someone is born that way. But I can't see it happening. I can't see Muslim homosexual imams, in the way that Christians have allowed gays into the Church. I can't see that happening in the mosque, in Islam. I hope it doesn't happen. I don't know what to say about the medical evidence. All I would say is that maybe the medical evidence is wrong, because God has spoken, so I accept what God has said.'

In any case, no matter what may be demonstrated to be the case in nature, religion has been given to us to help us transcend nature:

'Let us assume that it is twenty per cent of the population – I am going to assume that it is twenty per cent. Religion doesn't follow our instincts, religion supersedes our instincts, teaches our instincts, modifies our instincts. Men and women, human beings, behave in an instinctive way, which may be right, may be wrong, may be good, may be bad. But then comes religion which teaches what God wants us to do, and how to behave. We still have freedom of choice, how to behave. But religion says to us, no, this way is bad for you; or, yes, this way is good for you. So a homosexual who is feeling that way inclined is discouraged by religion from indulging. In other words, religion comes to modify the behaviour of the individual, and the individual is free to follow that teaching or not to do so at all. And that again is fair and reasonable.'

So even if homosexuality were 'in nature', homosexual acts would still be forbidden:

'If we accept that there are two natures, which at the extremes we can call a masculine characteristic and a feminine, Allah is not going to create us all with exclusively one of the two opposed extremities of these different characteristics. There is bound to be a spectrum. As a Muslim, I don't accept homosexuality in the way that I think it's understood. I don't believe it is acceptable. Certainly the sexual acts are not acceptable in Islam. However, I can understand – and I wouldn't find it hard to accept, if this research is confirmed – that there are certain people who straddle the spectrum, and are not clearly classed among the masculine traits or the feminine traits, but are somewhere in the middle. That does not mean that they cannot live a decent, normal life.'

JB: 'Does that mean that they may have a homosexual nature but cannot express it?'

'No, they can express their nature in whatever way it is allowed to be expressed.'

JB: 'But not in sexual acts?'

'No. You are not talking about men created with women's sexual organs, so that is not the issue. If we are still talking about a man created with all the physical manifestations of a man, then he must behave and use them in the way that God created them.'

But what if a man or a woman exercises that freedom of choice and engages in homosexual acts; granted that it will be condemned on the Day of Judgement, what should the attitude of the community be now?

'The Muslim position with regard to homosexuality is this: it is not allowed. It is not something that is good. It is prohibited and it is sinful. But what do you do about homosexuals who are practising in private somewhere, and you don't know of it? You certainly don't go and break the door down and say, "Oh, you're homosexual, you've got to be punished." You don't do that because in Islam you don't spy on people, and you don't enter without their permission. If people do whatever sinful thing they are doing, not just homosexuality but anything, in private and in secret, then nobody has the right to invade their privacy. But the trouble comes when it is advertised, when people who are homosexually inclined start to convince other people that it is all right to be homosexual. Of course it is not all right to be homosexual. It is not good for society. But if one or two people want to do it privately, then I have no right to invade their privacy. In any case, the sinfulness of homosexuality in Islam is not on the same level as the sinfulness of adultery, or of sex between two unmarried people. That is because marriage is easy – you enter into marriage easily, and adultery is forbidden in Islam because it takes away the rights of the woman. Islam concentrates so much on preserving the rights of women, and on preserving the good of society. So the sinfulness of homosexuality is not on the same level as adultery, and that is clear from the punishments which are described in the Qur'ān for each of them. The punishment for homosexuals is that you bother them until they stop. You say to them, "You silly people, you are doing a stupid thing." If they stop, you don't touch them, don't go near them, to remind them of what they did. So it's a very merciful religion, really.'

How Do Judgements and Interpretations Change?

In all these examples there is a clear and necessary conservation of the past and of the Tradition. Nevertheless, there is a continuing responsibility to interpret and test the position so far reached, not least because Islam *depends* on continuing argument and debate, not on a central authority which decides on behalf of all. Once again, it places extreme importance on the role of the ulama, and on *ijma'* (the community consensus):

'The deepest question here is the relationship between the imperative to believe in revelation and contemporary science, which of course necessarily changes in every age. I don't deny that there may well be divine imperatives which look scandalous, and I think that is actually an essential part of religion. I think it's only a modern, more or less Protestant, understanding of religion which thinks that religion is always necessarily humanistic, or must in some sense be domesticated. However, if there were substantial evidence for the view that for some people homosexuality is part of their nature (and to be fair, no scripture of the Hebrew tradition makes that distinction between acts and disposition), then I think it would count as a major theological puzzle. We would have a word of scripture which is supposed to be perfectly true and error-free, and yet we would be being asked to patronize an attitude which we cannot conscientiously adopt. So I think this would have to be an item on the agenda for the Muslims in their attempt to grapple with modernity. I wouldn't suggest that they dismiss it. It is a difficult question, how to look at the demands of revelation when they seem to conflict with humanly attainable evidence, which seems to go against it. So I wouldn't pronounce on it myself. This should be a question for the *ijma'* of the community; and they should decide this question in the light of considerations deriving from scripture, primarily, but also from what is in the contemporary world.'

JB: 'But then the question is obvious: how can Muslims reach a consensus given the divisions among them? When you talk of the *ijma'* of the community, of what community are you talking, Bradford or the world?'

'Obviously it would be tremendously immodest of me to speak of the world. *Ijma'* obtained in Bradford would not, I think, be recognized in Leeds or any other city. What is really meant here is any body of believers. If it was to have universal application it would have to come from a recognized seat of learning – al-Azhar in Egypt, for example. Bradford is not a seat of theological learning, so any *ijma'* here would be of no consequence to anyone outside. But on relatively minor matters, the community can simply get together and say, "We will adopt the following attitude on this particular point". So if someone asks, for example, about *halal* meat in schools – supposing they cannot get *halal* meat without undue inconvenience – are they then allowed to eat non-*halal* meat? Then it's up to the local community to decide. But it would have no universal validity for the house of Islam.'

Clearly, then, there is a major item here on the Muslim agenda for action. The diffused authority works well on minor matters. But how is the process towards consensus to be achieved when the house of Islam is, in *some* respects, divided against itself? An immediate answer is that absolute consensus in all matters is not in the least desirable. Islam depends on a dynamic relation between revelation and life, which in turn requires debate and disagreement, since otherwise the integrity of the human Caliphate (humans created, according to the Qur'ān, as the free but responsible agents of God on earth) would be compromised:

'Consultation is essential in a Muslim society. The Qur'ān

describes the Muslims as the people who decide on their affairs through consultation. In other words, participation in decision making is mandatory. To have decisions imposed from above is rejected very strongly in Islam, because it deprives the community of its essential quality of being a community of people who take part in decisions. Now, the emphasis on consultation implies that we do not agree. We do not consult with each other if we are all in agreement.

'The Qur'ān describes how this principle of consultation was enshrined after a defeat suffered by the Muslims at the battle of Uhud. At the battle of Uhud, the Prophet met with his companions in Medina. There was a huge army coming to attack and crush them in Medina itself. Now, the Prophet and the minority thought that the best plan for their campaign was to stay in Medina, because they were smaller in number: they would be able to protect themselves with the buildings, and fight a street battle; and they thought that this would give them the strategic advantage against their opponents, who would have no supplies, and of course would be in the open while the others would be safeguarded by the houses. But the majority thought it too humiliating to wait for the enemy. They must go out and fight, and the Prophet bowed to the decision of the majority. One of those in favour of staying in Medina was a man who really disliked Islam, and was not a Muslim at all. But he was under an obligation to help. He said, "Well, you rejected my advice, and I am such an important man, I am not going to fight with you." He abandoned them and took with him one third of the army. The battle started and the Muslims lost. Then, after the battle, the revelation came to the Prophet, saying to him, 'Consult them'. The Qur'ān says: Look, you've got to consult. Meet and consult, and once you've arrived at a decision, then move forward. So we have four stages: Put the question; argue

about it; decide; and then move and act. Once you have come to
the decision, unanimity must then be there.'

This is, in its way, the Muslim version of democracy:

'The absence of discussion in most of the Muslim states at
the present time is really a function of the system being
uncertain of itself, and of the leadership not being certain of its
legitimacy. My own belief is that the Muslim community in, for
example, Britain, will eventually learn to bring an interpretation
of Islam which is closer to the idea of consultation and of
arguing, which is the idea of *shura*, or what in the West might be
called, for want of any better word, democracy. And this version
of Islam, which would really be truer to the ideal of Islam, in
which you have discussion and dissent and arguments, and give-
and-take throughout the whole process, this version could
eventually return to the Muslim world. I have always believed
that if Muslims convert Western Europe, then the Muslim world
would be converted to Islam.'

But clearly it would be very different from existing
understandings of democracy, and for at least some Muslims who
reflect on the matter, this would be no bad thing:

'This is a very important question. The way I see it, in terms
of political theory, is that we have to find the right form of
government for attaining political humility. I think it is fair to say
that, although it has been a routine assumption of Western
thought that secular postures of power always lead to humility, I
don't think that they do – two major wars, Hiroshima, the
possibility of nuclear holocaust – none of these are patronized
by religious ambitions. These are all secular, nationalist
ambitions that people have had. The most incisive critiques of
the hubris of power have come from those concerned with
secularity and what it may do. In George Orwell's *1984*, Big
Brother is not a Muslim; he is not even an ayatollah. He is a

secular leader. So I think the Western critics and political theorists need to be very careful when they say that theocracy patronizes a peculiarly arrogant form of government. I don't think it does. I think it's an open question. You can't decide it on *a priori* grounds. There is no form of government which is not open to abuse, whether theocratic, dynastic or democratic.'

It is the combination of discussion and disagreement leading to a decision (sometimes local, sometimes extending to a much wider constituency) which creates the impression, to those who see only the end-term of the process, that Islam is dictatorial and repressive of freedom of opinion. In fact, even if the decision issues in the form of a fatwa it must rest on a consensus – although the status of a fatwa may differ in the two major communities of Islam:

'There is a basic difference in the Sunni and Shia approach here. The Shia approach is that, after the eleventh imam went, according to them, into hiding or vanished from human sight, that authority came to their imams, who can engage in *ijtihad*, that is, give their own opinion, and they can issue a fatwa and that becomes binding for all of them. But Sunnis do not believe in that. A fatwa is given by a mufti. *Mufti* is a particular title which is given to a person who knows Islamic jurisprudence extremely well and can give an opinion, but for all the Sunnis, the opinion has got to be corroborated. If one gives a fatwa and another gives a different fatwa, then it may be that the differences remain, as they do among the four schools. So, for example, they differ on deciding when a marriage has broken down and on the procedures for divorce.'

But the point still remains that if a decision or a fatwa does have warrant for itself, and is based on consultation and discussion, then it cannot be repudiated or ignored:

'The fatwa as such cannot be renounced by any person in

his clear mind, any more than you could ask the Pope to renounce any of the Ten Commandments, or the Chief Rabbi to renounce anything that is written in the Torah or the Talmud.'

But this again is to hear Muslims setting an agenda for themselves. If it is necessary to convert Europe in order that Muslims may then recover Islam as it was intended to be, based on discussion and respecting dissent, it implies that the present state of Islam is far from the ideal; and no Muslim we listened to disagreed with that. The speaker who talked of the *shura* as the Muslim version of democracy went on:

'Of course, I am talking of the theory, the principle. The practice can fail miserably to reach up to the ideals of Islam. For one thing, the Muslims are not in a political situation where they can *be* the umma. Regarding the current situation let me say that the Muslim states, all of them, are at the moment under the sway of what you may call Western concepts of the state. The nation-state is something that sits uncomfortably in a Muslim political system. We are a universal state essentially, and an all-embracing state, in the sense that the whole umma means every Muslim must be a citizen of one unified state. So the nation-state is an innovation, and we are not able to live with it very successfully. We have borrowed a lot also from the West – all that contributes to a totalitarian state: a more skilful police force, an electronic system of surveillance through which people know what other individuals are doing or thinking, and then also the control of the media.

'In every Muslim country the media is entirely in the hands of the state, so nobody, no other voice, no dissenting voice can be heard, except with a very few exceptions where the dissenting voice is allowed just a little leeway. So, in terms of politics we are all living, not in a democratic system in the sense that we usually understand it, nor in the sense that Islam perhaps intended to create with individuals participating with free discussion. Now this is a situation which Muslims feel very deeply, and the Muslim movements unfortunately have not grappled with this effectively. Most of the Muslim movements are in themselves a mirror image of the authorities which prevail in our society as well. So you find the Muslim organizations and the Muslim parties are just as authoritarian. If you challenge the leader, you are expelled straight away, rather than listened to. So you find this lack of freedom, this lack of participation in many Muslim countries, no doubt about it, and this is our crisis, our major problem.'

That is a clear statement of the imperative necessity for Muslims to recover in practice the means through which the vision of community, based on consensus and recognizing diversity, can be realized. Even before the Caliphate was abolished after the First World War, it no longer had the means to realize what in theory it was meant to be. With modern communications, these are now at hand. Whether the will exists to realize the umma as the community that transcends the nation-state is another matter. At least the theory is clear: Islam is not 'fixed' in the sixth, or in the ninth, century. It is open to movement and development as it encounters new circumstances and as it engages in continuing reflection on its own tradition. But if it encourages freedom of opinion, then how can a demand for the execution of Salman Rushdie receive so much support among Muslims? And how does a transcendent state deal with those who do not have a Muslim understanding of its relation to the non-Muslim world, and with those who disagree with it?

CHAPTER THREE

MUSLIMS AND NON-MUSLIMS:
THE STATE AND HOLY WAR, OTHER RELIGIONS, APOSTASY
AND TREASON

Muslim Communities and the Islamic State

There is no single voice of Islam, nor any single reality which can be identified as 'Islam'. As we have seen, there is nothing like a Pope or Vatican which can mimic secular institutions and can claim to speak as the only authentic and legitimate Muslim voice. But there is nevertheless an immense coherence and conformity of both Muslim belief and practice. *Any* Muslim voice has to be in conformity with the Qur'ān (open though the Qur'ān is to continuing interpretation), and it has to be in conformity with Hadith. But even the Hadith do not envisage all possible situations or circumstances that might arise in the present or future, and in any case, *abadith* are not all of equal status in Islam: there has been a long process of testing the authenticity of each Hadith; and that is a point, as we shall see, of real importance in assessing the Muslim treatment of apostates from Islam.

The Qur'ān plus Hadith plus continuing interpretation produced the schools of Sharia, but even among themselves they were different. Add to those differences of practical application of Islam to life the fact that, as Hampeté Ba once put it, 'Islam is

like water, taking on the colour of the ground it flows over'
(which amounts to enormous cultural accretion and variation),
and it can be seen that there may be profound unities in Islam,
but no unity:

'The Sharia is not an immutable body of doctrine. It's a very
complicated mix of materials which are derived from Scripture –
which is in fact invariant and can't be changed. Then there are
other things to do with Tradition, to do with *ijma'*, or consensus
of the community at any given time; and then of course there
may be individual learned authorities who may have a special
prominence and who may have to be taken into account. So it is
true that Islam is a law-centred faith. It certainly says that it has a
charter for human society, and that if men were to live it, then
the Kingdom of God, if you like to put it like that, would be
realized. But none of that precludes many different styles of
Islamic culture, nor does it preclude a reverent scepticism. A
reverent scepticism is not incompatible with Islam.'

But that recognition of the validity of many variations on
the Islamic theme does not endorse variations which have largely
or entirely abandoned Sharia. Here is the political crux. The
outsider may be alarmed by rumours or impressions of Islamic
practices which, as we have just seen with some specific
examples, would themselves be condemned by Sharia. Another
example, of painful importance to many women through the
world, is the practice of female circumcision; since this occurs
extensively in countries with Muslim majorities, can it be
assumed that this is a cultural accretion which Islam endorses?

'No. It is pre-Islamic, it is practised also by Christians in
those countries, and it is not any part of Muslim doctrine. It is
not a core-belief of Islam, it is a pre-Islamic practice.'

But the political crux is then obvious: how can Islam, as a
collective entity, protest against cultural accretions which are

contradictory to Islam? Or to put it another way, why are there no protests against a widespread practice of this kind as there are against Salman Rushdie? By what means can the 'charter for humanity' be realized, even among the Muslims themselves?

The problem of co-ordinated Muslim action has already been identified (see chapter 1) in the recognition that there is no Islamic state anywhere in the world today:

'It is obligatory on Muslims that they should set up an Islamic state, an independent and completely Islamic state. We've got some so-called Islamic states at the moment in the world, but they are not completely Islamic. There are some that approach it, some that are on the fringes of it, others that are distancing themselves even further from it. But there isn't one that is completely Islamic.'

JB: 'How do you know when a full Islamic state has come into being?'

'It is so clear what Islam requires that there is no difficulty. The Qur'ān and Hadith are so clear about what is required of a Muslim, what is required of a Muslim ruler, how a country should be ruled. It's all very, very clear. Anybody who knows what Islam says can see for himself what is an Islamic state and what is not.'

Of the countries on the edge of being truly Muslim states, Iran is the main candidate:

'I would recognize the Republic of Iran as an Islamic state, though personally I might differ on points of law with them. I think that the sincerity with which they apply Islam as they see it is there, and therefore I would recognize them as a Muslim state. I don't think I see any other country trying with as much sincerity as they are to apply Islamic law.'

But there are of course, as we saw in chapter 1, deep divisions between Sunni and Shia Muslims. So even in the case of Iran, it would still be a restricted understanding of the Islamic state:

'The nearest candidate in terms of Shiism is Iran. But the psychological flavour of Shiism is very different from Sunnism – for example, in the relation of Shias to their imam. Khomeini was a very charismatic figure, and not just because he was himself very charismatic, but because of the role which he played within the theology of Shiism, which Sunnism doesn't have: imams for Sunnis are imams: they lead the prayers; and there are the ulama who are very knowledgeable, but they don't have a direct line to divine messages. So the political reality will be very different in the two cases.'

Where Sunni Muslims are concerned, the recovery of Islam and the possibility of concerted Muslim action would involve the restoration of the Caliphate. Under the Ottoman empire, which came to an end after the First World War, the Caliph offered at least a theoretical symbol of unity:

'The Caliphate represents the decision of all individual Muslims as to who should lead them. In that respect, there is a democratic process (but keeping the word "democratic" in inverted commas) by which a person can be nominated to lead the community, and he must set up also a body of people around him who can advise him on how best to lead the community. The central concern of this caliphate is the maintenance of the sovereignty of God and the maintenance of the values of Islam, so that Muslims as well as non-Muslims can live together in peace. *Khalifa* means "trusteeship", or "stewardship". It carries with it a responsibility in everyday life, that we are entrusted with creation, and as trustees, through revelation, God provides us with the guidelines to fulfil that trust. This is embodied in a body of beliefs, values and norms, which constitute knowledge. The individual Muslim, as well as the community, represents this *khalifa*, this trusteeship. This does not mean that this position is not held by other human beings. All human beings, whether they are conscious of it or not, or whether they accept it or not, are *khalifas* of God. Those who are conscious of it and are prepared to take up the responsibility enter the Islamic theological map.

'So this is one reason why we must make a distinction between a Muslim country and an Islamic state. An Islamic state is one which is at peace and is trying to realize the values that God is asking us to live by. Now there are countries which are Muslim states only in the sense that the vast majority of the population happens to be Muslim. But they have to be distinguished from an Islamic state where there is a conscious effort to realize the Sharia. In my opinion many of the problems being faced by Muslims and Muslim countries, and by Muslim minority groups, arise because the Sharia is not in operation. It is Sharia which protects individual Muslims and provides them with their rights against a powerful state, and which protects the rights of minorities against a large community of Muslims as well as against the state itself.'

But that only emphasizes the dilemma of collective Muslim action in achieving Sharia now:

'At this moment, that's very difficult, because we do not have a united Caliphate. A Caliphate is a body which is responsible for seeing that the trusteeship of the community as a whole is realized. There are certain decisions which cannot be made on an individual basis, such as war. They can only be made through the process of the Caliphate. Muslims no longer have that. The last Caliphate was during the Ottoman empire, which came to an end in 1921, or thereabouts. Since then Muslims have organized themselves, because of nationalism, on the basis of individual countries. So at this moment in time, Muslims can only find support from individual nation-states, but not from the totality of the one billion Muslims who now reside on this planet, because there is no single entity to which they can appeal. But of course contemporary Muslims are concerned with this, and that is why you find a variety of struggles going on across the Muslim world. Muslims are feeling both spiritually and psychologically that they have to realize this Caliphate again, if they are to tackle the manifest problems which they and humanity face.'

This is the paradox of incapacity: Islam is indeed simple, and it has, theoretically, the means to form part of the resistance movement against all that threatens human flourishing, which is the dynamic of other religions, at their best, as well. But once Islam was overrun by colonialism and was subordinated to the European nation-state (often with the creation of new states and boundaries), the dream of umma, of the single human community and family, became remote, and indeed, it began to come into conflict with patriotic loyalties to one's own territory and nation. In a way, this basic political fact – the incompatibility between the concept of the umma and the imposed nation-state – is the key to understanding the tensions and conflicts of the Muslim world today.

That became dramatically clear in Saddam Hussein's invasion and seizure of Kuwait – or of what to him and other Iraqis has long been a part of a single territory. As his announcement of the merger put it: 'What has befallen other states in the Arab lands befell Iraq when colonialism divested it of a dear part of itself, namely Kuwait . . . and thus kept part of its people and part of its wealth away from the origin and the well-spring.'

The reaction in the West was to make its usual error of construing the concepts of another culture in the grammar of its own tradition. It saw Saddam Hussein as a European dictator of the 1930s. In that way it handed back the initiative to Saddam Hussein, and made it seem possible that a concerted, albeit self-destructive, strike against Palestine/Israel might after all occur. For the West handed to Hussein two profoundly emotional concepts with which to rally at least some support to himself. The irony is that, although the two concepts are of powerful appeal in the Arab and Muslim world, there was no chance that the Arabs or other Muslims would respond to them until the West, by their misunderstandings, gave the opportunity to him.

The first and explicit concept is that of *'urubiyya,* of being Arab. The announcement already quoted began: 'Oh zealous Arabs everywhere, scarce are the days when the Arabs are jubilant. This has been the situation of the Arabs for the long time in which the foreigner reigned.' The concept of 'being Arab' is not essentially a matter of geography; it is a matter of belonging to the first community in which the word of God – in Arabic – was transmitted through Muhammad. It is a matter of academic argument how far the concept of *'urubiyya* (Arabism) prevailed before the time of Muhammad. In the Qur'ān, the Arabs (i.e. desert dwellers) appear as reprehensible land pirates: 'The Arabs are the most adamant in refusing belief, and in hypocrisy' (ix. 98).

All the more remarkable, therefore, was their transformation in virtually a single generation to those whose loyalty was no longer to a tribe or a kinship group, but to an entirely new vocation – to the new transcendental community brought into being by Islam. This is the second, and even more profound, concept, which is the controlling metaphor in the Islamic world. It is the concept of umma, of community. There is no concept more important for understanding the political world of Islam than this. It derives directly from the first experience of

Muhammad in the cave of Mount Hira, when he realized with overwhelming certainty, that if God is God, then it is God that God is. All or nothing. From that unity (*tawhid*) all other unities flow, including the unity of the whole human population as a single umma under God – with all the obligations and responsibilities which go with that.

Few things can be more destructive of the political and economic vision, summarized in the controlling metaphor of umma, than the imposition of the nation-state, emerging during the nineteenth century from Western political history. That is why the appeal of Saddam Hussein was immensely strong when he claimed: 'The spiteful pencil and scissors of imperialism began to draw up maps, based on ensuring that every part of the Arab homeland . . . will remain weak and ineffective towards Arab awakening [i.e. *'urubiyya*] and unity as a whole [i.e. umma]'. It is obvious that at the moment umma is not a controlling, but a dead, metaphor. As Muslims have been pointing out repeatedly in this book, there is not a single Islamic state anywhere in the world today, let alone a transcendental sense of umma. Where the Arabs are concerned, this is partly because some among them have an interest in preserving the boundaries of their own nation-states (many of which are extremely recent innovations), particularly where oil wealth is involved. So the appeal of Saddam Hussein had as much chance initially of being responded to as the cry of an imperialist to restore the British empire. But equally, there was no possibility either that he would have invaded Saudi Arabia. Despite the anger that some Muslims feel about the way in which the Saudis manage the most holy places of Islam which are located in their territory, there was no chance that Saddam Hussein would invade holy ground and thus alienate the conceptual (and emotional) support on which he had relied. The West, by failing to recognize this and by failing, therefore, to wait for a pan-Arab force to be established, returned the initiative to Saddam Hussein in a way that will prolong not only the conflict, but also the memories of what has been done to Arabs and to Islam in the past, in this conflict and in the years leading up to it.

This is not to say that Saddam Hussein will prevail – the least likely of all scenarios, particularly since some of his Muslim neighbours do not see him as a hero and seem to be feeling that if he has to be opposed, better now than later. The Arabs do not need the West to teach them to differentiate between right and wrong. What the West needs to learn from this episode is not how to deploy misplaced rhetoric derived from the 1930s, but how to listen to the conceptual language of a community which constitutes a quarter of the world's population. It is a language being spoken very clearly by the king of Jordan; but the West has already abused him for not singing its own tune. If the West were to work with that language, and not against it, it would help Arabs to achieve at last what the wasted years of Western diplomacy have been stifling. The language of umma is the language of transcendental community – precisely what the pressures on the planet most urgently require us to find. It is not an unrealistic idealism: it has, in fact, been realized in the past; it could be realized again, in the present, particularly if other traditions understand and endorse it. As matters stand at present, the post-colonial inheritance of imposed boundaries and novel loyalties is playing as much havoc here as in Africa:

The biggest obstacle to the realization of the dream of umma is this whole business of national sovereignties. We now have these nation-states. Of course, there are already pan-Islamic, or universalistic, movements, made up of people who want to put the fact of their being a Muslim above the fact of their being an Egyptian or of their being a Pakistani, and so on.

So this is clearly something that is going to be on the agenda indefinitely, because it hasn't been achieved yet. But I think there is a potential for it to be achieved. It depends on whether or not the Muslims are prepared to subdue the cultural details of their religion to the scriptural details of their religion. If they say, "Look, my being a Pakistani or my being an Egyptian is in some sense an accident of birth and biography, but my being a Muslim is a matter of God's grace," then I think it's quite easy to see that there is real potential for universal community.'

The Conversion of the Non-Muslim World

If this *were* to be achieved, it would be a political fact as momentous as the collapse of Communism in Eastern Europe. But does it imply, in any case, a necessary endeavour to bring the whole world into the domain of Islam? If, as we have heard repeatedly, the way forward for Islam is the way back to Sharia, which includes the institutional means of that recovery, does that also involve a commitment to the conquest or conversion of the rest of the world – as it would seem to do, if Islam is indeed God's charter for His world? Or to be more precise, is it an obligation for Muslims even now (short of the recovery of Islam) to try to become the majority? Here again the answers were unanimous:

'Oh yes, indeed. This is a very important thing. We have the concept of jihad [see pp. 84ff], which is much misunderstood in the West. jihad means "striving", in this case to spread Islam. But that does not mean by the sword so much as by the word and by example. So you will find that every true Muslim is always a missionary. So we try to convert the world. Our concept of the world and of the end of the world (in the sense of the objective) is to have one state, one religion and one umma –

the umma being the religious community. So we want to convert the world. That is our objective.'

'Everybody, at least if he is a generous person and is not a miser (and we are not encouraged to be misers as Muslims) and who has something valuable, would like to share it with other people. That's a natural human instinct. For us there is nothing more valuable than the divine guidance as it is put to us in the Qur'ān and in the Sunna of the Prophet. Naturally, we would want to share it with other people. It is for the benefit of all, it would provide the solutions to all the numerous problems which we face today. Naturally, we will acquaint other people with these possible solutions. There is no compulsion in Islam. But if people realize that these solutions are better solutions, they will take them on board, they will vote for them, and then if a majority of people in this country should be of that opinion, naturally we would develop into an Islamic state. If not, we will continue as we are, as long as there is a mutual respect and a tolerant attitude towards religion, tolerance based on justice, because you cannot divorce the two.'

'It is an obligation on us to spread our message. I don't mean in the sense of knocking on doors and handing out leaflets, but in letting people know what we believe, and in that if we see beliefs that are very contradictory, pointing out why we feel that they are wrong, and why people shouldn't believe or do that. I don't see why any groups, whether they are religious, like Hindus, or not, like communists, or atheists, should have anything to fear in that from Muslims.'

But then, why is Salman Rushdie hiding for his life? To that there is a particular answer, as we shall see. But in more general terms, what might the fear be to which that reference is made? Obviously, at root, a lack of symmetry. There is a clear fear that Muslim minorities may be accepted or welcomed in countries where they will, not surprisingly, insist on the same rights being accorded to them as to all other citizens. But if or when they become the majority, they will at once restrict corresponding freedoms for non-Muslims. It is what might be called the fear of the cuckoo in the nest. But a Muslim in Bradford countered that image with another:

'I would give the example of the owl and the parrot. The owl is considered to be a very wise and ingenious bird in the West. The perception of the owl is totally different in the East. If you go to India or Pakistan or Japan, the same bird is considered the most stupid bird that there is. If you call someone an owl in India, you have cursed them very badly. The same thing applies to the parrot. While the West feels that the parrot is very foolish, it just repeats things one after the other, the perception in the East is totally different. These images and opinions arise because of misunderstanding, because of lack of information or whatever. It is not true of Islam that it would eliminate minorities.'

The Domain of Islam and the Domain of War

But is this fear, or at least this perception of Islam as competitive and aggressive, really based on ignorance and misunderstanding? Islam has, after all, traditionally divided the world into *dar al-Islam* and *dar al-Harb*, the domain or the house of Islam, and the domain or the house of conflict or war. Does that polarization of the world still obtain as a living category of discrimination?

'In a way, yes; at least in the sense that we oppose governments who throw their weight behind bankers, trying to corrupt the resources and wealth of some nations, by insisting on the interest system. I am not advocating that war here means literally war. It means a state of caution. However, as is well

81

known, war in Islam is only permitted in defence and not in attack. But just as the last two world wars were not fought entirely for high principles, but were fought also for very strong economic interests, so now: the immoral eagerness to acquire wealth and subdue people has brought the world lots of suffering. Third World countries are weighted down with debts which they cannot repay. The Islamic principle is to repay the capital but not the interest. But the interest now exceeds the capital by many, many times. Insisting on payment and threatening to take the land is a kind of aggression, and Islam would resist it.'

For other Muslims, even that modified understanding of the two domains is no longer viable in the modern world, where interests and institutions are now so entangled, nor could it technically be bought into being:

'It is very difficult now to make such a distinction, because there is no Islamic state as such. The first condition for an Islamic state is that it must have a *khalifa*. The second condition is that the Sharia must be upheld. The third condition is that the instruments of the Sharia must be available to its citizens. These three conditions are not being met at the moment by any Muslim country. Therefore it is very difficult to make this distinction today, between *dar al-Islam* and *dar al-Harb*. After all, there are countries now which are not Muslim, whose values nevertheless enable Muslims to live their lives much, much more as Muslims than would be possible in some parts of the Muslim world. Within the Islamic faith there is no harm in that, because, I must remind you, there is a very important saying of the Prophet that for the Muslim the whole world is a *masjid* [literally, place of prostration, hence the usual word for mosque], in that the whole world is at the disposal of the Muslim. Wherever Muslims feel that they can practise their faith to the best of their ability, trying to uphold the ideals of the faith, they are free to live there.'

Even were the traditional categories to be retained, the fact is almost always overlooked that there is a *third* category, which is much more pervasive and applicable at the present time:

'In the past, the relationship between the Muslim state and the non-Muslim state was based on what was prevailing at the time: potentially, one was at war with the outside world. So the Muslim scholars divided the world into the two states, one the abode of peace (that is, the land of Islam), and the other the abode of war (that is, the land of non-Muslims). That was the concept. In the ancient world, the Roman empire acted in exactly the same fashion: there was the *pax Romana* in their own domain, and as for the outside, it was always at war with it. But in modern times this is no longer possible. Therefore, you have to come to an understanding. And again – because the Muslim jurists always had a tremendous imagination – this was foreseen. You find that the Shaffii school of law says, "No: the world is not divided into just two categories. There is another one, a third one, the land of agreement, or of covenant [i.e. *dar-as-Sulh*]." If you have an agreement with a particular state, then you are at peace with that state, regardless of its religion. We cannot have the situation as in the past.

'In any case, the law of nations (dividing the world) was devised by our scholars. They tried to relate it to original concepts of the Prophet, or to certain statements of the Qur'ān, but really, it was their own idea, and it can be pushed aside and new laws can be brought in. Now, it is true that we have a state of war with the world, but it is a war of ideology. If you have a mission to convert the world, then you are at war with all the ideologies which are opposed to you. But that is different from the war that used to be enshrined in our legal system, that you have peace here and war elsewhere. That has to go and it has already gone: almost all the Muslim states subscribe to the United Nations, and to international law as it now prevails, and they sign a lot of treaties and agreements, which shows a realism which is basic to Islam.'

Holy War

But the war of ideology nevertheless remains. And that immediately raises the even more fundamental concept (because it is in the Qur'ān) of jihad, mentioned earlier. Jihad is usually translated as 'holy war', but it has a more complex meaning than that, arising from the Arabic word *jahada*, 'he made an effort'. The underlying sense is one of 'striving':

'The Arabic word means "to strive in the cause of God". There are then many ways you can strive: using your mouth, explaining to people what Islam means; with your wealth, by giving to the orphans, or, for example, giving your money to Afghanistan. But the jihad that everyone knows about is the physical one, giving your life to God. There can be no greater jihad than that, when you give your whole life to God.'

JB: 'How strong is the obligation to engage in that physical jihad?'

'If Muslims are in a state of war, then it is compulsory. There is an incident in the Prophet's life when they had all gone out to a battle, but three men remained behind, making excuses – such as "My dates have to be harvested." The Prophet was furious: he wouldn't speak to them, he wouldn't allow Muslims to have anything to do with them till they died, because it was such a serious issue. So it is compulsory for a Muslim man: if there is defensive jihad going on in his locality, he is not allowed to hold back.'

Although the greatest possible jihad is the laying down of one's life in a war in defence of Islam, what is known as the greater jihad is, paradoxically, the warfare within oneself:

'A Muslim is in a state of jihad all the time. But the greater jihad is against oneself, against the evil impulses in oneself, against the tendencies towards idolatries – that is, the elevation of non-spiritual and non-divine things to the chief status in one's soul or one's heart. In circumstances where one is talking about resisting some kind of exterior evil, one still retains the personal struggle against the evil impulses within, including those impulses which might provoke one toward conflict when it is not strictly necessary. The Qur'ān advises us to speak kindly with unbelievers, and to argue and discuss with them. But when it is a matter of military threat, or a threat of death to a community or to an individual, then one must defend one's life.'

So the idea of jihad is most important when it is internalized:

'The greater jihad is the fight within yourself, the lesser jihad is the warfare outside. Of course you defend your territory, both physically and psychologically. But war or struggle is not just violence; it is also our having to realize, all the time, the greater common ground among us all. My goodness me, we've really got to come back to that, to all of us being human beings, all of us being the creation of the divine – we all come from the divine, we all return to the divine. But if you take the idea of war in terms of converting people to my faith – that's a tradition in Islam. Indeed, one of my ancestors was sent by the Sultan of Turkey to South Africa to convert the heathen, both Christians and Blacks. I am at odds with that because it is your conscience – you will develop it and it is not for me to change it, and that is not unIslamic. Therefore, if you're a good Jew, be a good Jew; if you're a good Buddhist, be a good Buddhist. It's not for me to change you.'

But the fact remains that the literal and lesser jihad still exists as an obligation, and that it can mean actual war although the circumstances of its occurrence are strictly controlled. Several of those to whom we spoke gave examples of situations where jihad in its sense of actual warfare is justified:

'I can give you two examples: one is the Lebanon. Here we see human beings – whether they are Christians, Muslims or whatever – in the worst form of human degradation. Women have to pick up food from the streets to feed their children; human dignity is at its lowest level. Islam cannot tolerate this situation. It is therefore the responsibility of Muslims outside Lebanon to try to help these people. This is where jihad comes in, to defend their nobility and dignity as human beings. The first step in this is to identify the causes of the problem. Let us say – and we know this to be the case – that outside influences are playing a part, and that those influences are so strong that merely articulating a concern for those people is not enough; it then may require something tougher, because human life is at stake. In that case, the Qur'ān allows for killing, if that is the only way of protecting human values. In the case of the Lebanon, it would mean that Muslims as a community (and it has to be the community; it cannot be an individual decision) would have to decide that the only way of retrieving the values and the sovereignty of God in that situation is that the community must go to war. Another example is Afghanistan. Here we had a superpower invading a smaller nation and trying to replace its government. The people have the right, in the framework of jihad, to defend themselves by whatever means they see fit. And they have the right to call upon Muslims outside Afghanistan to assist them, provided the Muslims outside believe that they have a legitimate case.'

How far, then, might the phrase 'by whatever means' be taken?

If it means literal war, it is clear that extreme restrictions apply. When Muhammad commissioned an army to resist an invasion from the Byzantine empire, he is reported to have said:

'In avenging the injuries inflicted upon us, do not harm the non-belligerents in their homes; spare the weakness of women; do not injure infants at the breast, nor those who are sick. Do not destroy the houses of those who offer no resistance; and do not destroy their means of subsistence, neither their fruit trees, nor their palms.'

Exactly the same is reported of Abu Bakr, the first Caliph or successor of Muhammad:

'If Allah gives you victory, do not abuse your superior position, and do not stain your swords with the blood of one who surrenders. Do not touch the children, the women, or the infirm . . . Do not cut down the palms or other fruit trees, do not destroy the products of the earth, ravage no fields, burn no houses . . . Treat the prisoners and he who throws himself on our mercy with pity, as Allah shall do to you in your need.'

So there are limits on the means to be employed in jihad. But also Muslims should not be frightened of the weapons or excesses of enemies who threaten life or threaten Islam:

'Theoretically, in relation to jihad, there should be no circumstances where Muslims are being persecuted to the extent that they have been in Eastern Europe. Diplomatic efforts should be made first, but if it comes to it, then there should be actual conflict. The word *jihad* encompasses all these efforts. It isn't just fighting. It is any exertion to right a wrong. In practice, we don't have the unified voice to do this. But in theory, it is clear what should be done. The Muslim community is like a body: if one part of that body is suffering from any ailment, the rest of the body must go to its rescue.'

JB: 'What if those who are causing the ailment are possessed of nuclear weapons? Do you have a jihad against an atom bomb?'

'In Afghanistan we have had the situation where the jihad was declared against the Russians, and Russia does hold nuclear weapons. That is not something which should frighten us. I don't believe that Islamic beliefs will ever allow us to develop a nuclear bomb, because we cannot kill indiscriminately. But we would fight against someone who possesses such weapons. There is a possibility that they might not use it anyway, but that's not the point. If there is injustice, and we have any power to stop that injustice, it is our duty to do that.'

JB: 'So if Pakistan were to develop a nuclear arsenal, that would contradict Islam?'

'It definitely contradicts Islam, just as their development in the West contradicts Christianity.'

It follows that the development by Israel of its own nuclear weapon system may not be the deterrent that it is supposed to be.

'There was a true jihad being fought in Afghanistan. That looks as though one day it will be a Muslim state. Palestine has its on and off days: sometimes it looks as though, yes, we can have a jihad, we can defeat the Jews; on other days, as with the *intifada*, we think, no, that's going to remain a dream. But it could happen.'

But what jihad certainly cannot mean is a general warfare against the world for its conquest and conversion. There must indeed be a hope that all people will be converted, but there cannot be compulsion in religion; and a Muslim living in a non-Muslim country must accept the laws of the country that he or she is in, provided they are not aggressive against Islam.

'If we are living in a state where we have entered into an agreement with the government, as we have in a way with the British government, then we have agreed to live by the rules and regulations here as long as they don't prevent us from practising our faith; and the bargain on our side is that we accept what this government deems to be the law. That means toleration of other communities. We have an obligation to pass on the message of what we believe to other people. In any non-Muslim country we feel that we should be allowed to spread these beliefs freely. If they forbade us, then we would have to declare a state of jihad against that country. But if a country says, as England does, that you are free to live here and you are free to talk about Islam, and to spread Islam as much as you want, then we would have in a sense a treaty with that country.'

The Protected People of the Book

The relation of Islam to non-Muslim religions is governed by one basic, non-negotiable verse of the Qur'ān, which states that there is no compulsion in religion: 'As regards those who do not fight against you because of your religion and do not drive you out of your homes, God does not forbid you to treat them with goodness and to be just to them' (lx. 8). The word for 'goodness' is *birr*, which points to a stability of relationship which is beyond even justice: it is the word used to describe a Muslim's duties to his or her parents. It issues in the Qur'ānic statement: 'For you there is your religion, for me there is my religion' (cix. 6). In practice this is exactly what we find Muhammad doing: when he drew up an agreement with the Jews in Medina (part of the so-called Constitution of Medina), he said, 'To Muslims their religion, to Jews their religion.' Equally, there is no doubt of the severity of the measures taken by Muhammad against those who were perceived as threatening to attack or destroy Islam, including a number of Jewish tribes. But Muslims can only take such action in defence. They cannot otherwise take any initiative against adherents of another religion:

'Muslims are not going to invade the world like barbaric hordes. Islam is not like that. Islam has such a great respect for other people as communities. Islam is the only religion that introduced this idea of the *dhimmis* [non-Muslims in Muslim countries under Muslim protection] and of the *ahl al-Kitab* ["People of the Book" – any community that has received the revelation from God as Scripture], so that we are required to treat them with respect. A Muslim man can marry a Christian or a Jewess. Can a Jew marry a Muslim woman and allow her to remain in her faith? No. Islam is the only religion that has been so tolerant to others. Until the 1940s we had a great Muslim empire, the Ottoman empire. It was only because of the First World War that the Islamic empire came to an end. It lasted four or five hundred years. No other empire, no other religion on earth, has lasted the way that Islam has, because it is so tolerant. We don't force people to become Muslims. We may ask them to come under our political control, if we are the rulers, but we would never force anyone to become Muslim. In Spain, for example, the Jews had their Golden Age under the Muslims. They did not have it under Israeli leadership or Christian leadership or under the Nazis, they had it under Islam. The age they remember is the age under the Muslims in Spain.'

The Qur'ān recognizes that there were many prophets before Muhammad, particularly among the Jews (of whom Jesus was one). The fact that Jews and Christians are now divided from each other only illustrates that they both perverted the qur'āns entrusted to them for their own purposes. Nevertheless, they are *ahl al-Kitab* who have a special status and protection under Islam (so that it is a matter of real practical importance who counts as being 'a People of the Book', as we shall see):

'*Ahl al-Kitab* means literally "People of the Book", and it means Judaism and Christianity and other recognized religions, in the sense that God did send down Scripture to Jesus and he did send down Scripture to Moses. What happened was that they deviated from their own Scriptures; they stopped following the actual commandments of God and changed their religions. However, since their foundations are still in the Word of God, we do not reject them completely and say, "These are *kafirs* [rejecters], these are non-Muslims." They are to be accorded respect.'

JB: 'Hindus also believe that they have received revelation from God as Scripture. Do they count as People of the Book?'

'Various scholars like to say that they do. But if you look at the Hadith of the Prophet, it is very, very clear that he only talks about Jews and Christians, and about Jesus and Moses and various other prophets. The Hindu leaders are not mentioned. We do not accept that God gave them a Scripture.'

JB: 'But the Qur'ān is related to the circumstance in which Muhammad lived, and in which he was in constant interaction with Jews and Christians. So the Qur'ān does not mention many things – Outer Mongolia, for example; can you not apply the provisions of the Qur'ān to people not specifically mentioned?'

'Everything happens with the permission of God and the will of God. Nothing can happen if God does not want it to happen. If God wanted to reveal something about them, he could have done. He wanted the circumstances to happen that did happen so that what he wanted could be revealed. As I say, some scholars do argue that Hindus should be included. An important point is that a Muslim man can marry a woman who is one of the People of the Book. That is allowed for the Jews and

Christians, and some have allowed it for the Hindus. I feel that it is restricted in the Qur'ān to the two people, Jews and Christians, and that we should not take it further. The other important thing is the way in which they can live by their own tradition under Muslim law. But that is already extended, in that anyone who is not a Muslim, whether Hindu, Jew or Christian, is allowed to live in their own way as they pay the *jizya* [special tax, in return for protection]. The Hindus would not suffer as a result.'

The Status of Christians

Christians, of course, raise particular problems for Muslims, because they hold beliefs which are deeply contradictory to Islam at some of its most profound points. Thus *ash-Shahada* proclaims that there can only be God in the case of God, there cannot be more than one God, and anyone who claims that there is is a *mushrik*: one who commits the offence of *shirk*, of associating something with God that is not God, and there can scarcely be a more serious offence in Islam. Yet Christians claim that God is three persons, albeit constituting a single Being: are they *mushrikun?*

'According to the Muslims, yes. Although they end up saying that it is one God, the Muslims nevertheless have an ambivalent attitude towards them, as also because of the ambiguity of the Trinity itself. However, the ambiguity itself has to be taken into account, so that Muslims say, Well, they're almost *mushrikun*; but they are still put under the title of *ahl al-Kitab*. But we feel that their elevation of Christ to the position of a God is something that we cannot accept, and we do not accept it. Christ is a human being, and beyond this we cannot go.'

It is equally outrageous to Muslims for the claim to operate

92

the other way around, that in Christ God united human nature to his own:

'As a Muslim I have to regard that as a mistake, an error, which Christians have made, but certainly not an error great enough to restrict them from entering heaven. We are told in the Qur'ān that anyone who has a sincere faith in his Creator (and then it mentions the Christians and the Jews) will enter Paradise – or they will have no fear. I think there's a lot of confusion in Christianity anyway about what the Trinity represents. There are those with whom I've spoken who almost openly admit that it is a Trinity of Gods – three Gods: they do believe in three separate powers. Others I've spoken to (and that's the vast majority) strongly say that it is one power, that we believe in one Creator. And that is what we accept as Muslims as being the basis of the Christian faith; and we are told in the Qur'ān that this is enough for us to accept them. Judaism is even more direct, so there is no problem.'

But Christians claim even further that the death of Jesus on the Cross was necessary for the redemption of the world and for our rescue from sin and death. However, according to the Qur'ān (iv. 156/7), Jesus did not die on the Cross at all: God rescued his faithful prophet, and substituted for Jesus an appearance only (the Arabic of the Qur'ān can in fact be translated in a way that is coherent with the Christian belief that Jesus died on the Cross, but no Muslim reads the Arabic that way). There seems here to be an even more radical divide:

'As a matter of history, it is not possible to know [whether Jesus did or did not die on the Cross]. It is highly confused, with many different accounts. As a matter of religion, I think that it is perhaps necessary for Christians to believe in a crucifixion and a resurrection, because for Christians it is necessary for salvation and for the redemption of humanity. But for Muslims such an act is not necessary. We do not believe in original sin, for example, which I see as the beginning which leads inevitably to the necessity for a Messiah to be sacrificed, as in Christianity Christ was. For Muslims, there was no original sin. Everybody is born as a child of God and as a sinless and pure spirit. As we grow up and as we mature and gain spiritual understanding and responsibility, then the choice about our own path of salvation is in our own hands. There are some individuals who never reach that stage – they are, for example, retarded – and they remain in that state of childhood and therefore they remain sinless. No matter what they do, they remain sinless, because they do not have the spiritual responsibility of an adult.'

JB: 'But that means that Christians are a living contradiction of Islam, because they are living an account of human nature which is false.'

'Perhaps, yes. As a Muslim I do feel that it is not spiritually fruitful for me to think of individuals as born in sin, and as needing an active redemption of the kind claimed in the crucifixion and resurrection. The Emperor of China had something to say on the matter, when some missionaries were trying to convince him of the truth of the Christian message, and he said: "Well, if God so loved the world, why did he leave China in darkness for so long?".'

Despite the contradiction and errors, Christians nevertheless remain People of the Book. It follows that they should be allowed, in Muslim countries, to follow their own *din*, or lifeway, without restriction, provided only that they do not proselytize or become missionaries:

'Every Muslim state has its own attitude, which is usually built upon its experiences in the past. Many Muslim countries are concerned about Christian missionary endeavour, and that has shaped their attitudes in terms of what they allow such minorities to do. But from my own knowledge of the Middle East and other Muslim countries, nearly all of them have allowed religious minorities, particularly Christians, to have their own places of worship. I am not sure where, for example, in Saudi Arabia a Christian can go and worship in a church, but I know that in the Gulf states, which have a long history of Christian contact, Christians have their own churches; in some cases they have their own bishops, even, and they are free to worship. What Muslim countries are wary about, because of the long history of missionary activity, is the role of mission.'

There seems to be, in that position, another example of a lack of symmetry – in the sense that Muslims have claimed the right to be missionary themselves in non-Muslim countries. But again, it is important to bear in mind that these rules can only apply in a true Islamic state, of which, as we have heard repeatedly, there are no examples at the present time:

'So far as the duty of a Christian is concerned, his or her duty is to be a missionary, wherever he or she is. That is from the Christian point of view. From the Muslim point of view, it is his or her duty as a Muslim to be a missionary, wherever he or she is. How it is put into effect depends on the policy followed in any particular country. If it is policy in England to support complete freedom of missionary activity, as it is, then that is all right. It means that England is not a religious state. In the same way, Bangladesh is not a religious state, although it says that Islam is now declared to be the state religion. But it is not a religious state, so it allows Christian missionaries to do their work, and that is all right too.'

All this is extremely clear. It would, for example, be a contradiction of Islam if a Christian bishop were not allowed to travel freely in his overseeing of Christian congregations, provided he was not attempting to subvert Islam:

'Any Muslim leader would tell you the same, that a Christian bishop has the right to visit the Christian communities, in whatever country they are, if they are of the same denomination, and to participate with them in their celebrations. We had the example of the Pope visiting Morocco just a short while ago. There was no outcry of the ulama against the visit.'

In principle, Christians should be as free to build churches in Saudi Arabia as Muslims are free to build mosques in London:

'I am sure that can be allowed, because that was allowed in the Prophet's time. The Jews and Christians were allowed to worship in their own ways.'

JB: 'So if Christians anywhere in a country with a Muslim majority were experiencing pressure against themselves, or were not allowed to build a church for their own congregation, that would be a contradiction of Islam?'

'Oh yes, I am sure that the ruler would be required to stop, because Jews and Christians are allowed to worship in the ways they want. If that doesn't happen, it is because of ignorance.'

JB: 'But who requires a ruler to stop?'

'God does. It is set down in the Qur'ān and the Hadith how judges, and how rulers, are supposed to behave. It is very clear. So they would have to do it without anyone explaining it to them. But if the rulers are not behaving in an Islamic manner, then the people must tell them to do so. We see that happening all the time after the Prophet's death: the Caliphs were holding office in the mosque, and women and men would get up and say, "That's wrong", very rudely sometimes to the great Caliphs; they would say, "The Prophet did it like this". And the Caliph would say, in a very abashed way, "I am so sorry".'

Of course, being realistic, there is no possibility of a church or synagogue being built in the holy places of Islam. It would be like building a mosque in the middle of the Vatican. But that does not affect the general point:

'You should not compare Saudi Arabia with the whole of Britain. You should compare it with the Vatican. Do you allow Muslim services in the Vatican? Would you allow a mosque to be built in St Peter's Square? When we have a mosque there, then we'll have a church in Mecca.'

JB: 'But there might well be a mosque in Rome; do you compare the whole of Saudi Arabia with the Vatican?'

'I would, yes. This is a place that is particularly holy to the Muslims. The earth is not so small that you have to go to the desert of Saudi Arabia and insist on making a church. That would be a provocative act. However, there are Christians working in Saudi Arabia, and those people have every right to worship in whatever manner they want. And not only can they do so, they do. I would invite you to go to Egypt and see the Egyptian Copts who have many more rights than Muslims anywhere, on television, on radio and in public, to express their views. I would be very happy, as a Muslim living in England, to get half the rights that the Copts have got in Egypt.'

The Status of Hindus

All that discussion of freedom to worship as one wants had particular reference to the People of the Book – those who have revelation from God, no matter how much they have corrupted it. What of a religion whose worship seems, at least at first sight, to contradict Islam at an even more sensitive spot? What of religion which appears to set up images of God, both male and female, and to worship them? What of Hinduism? Is not Islam committed to an unremitting warfare against idolatry?

'Worshipping idols is disgusting, because it is an insult to Almighty God, who created us, if idols are being worshipped instead of Him. But we would not go around breaking the idols. Nor did we do so when we had the great Mogul dynasty in India. Hinduism was not suppressed. We had the power to do so if we wanted, but we allowed them to continue. All we could do was to tell Hindus – and tell Muslims as well – not to fall into the trap. But we would not force them, and we would not go round smashing the idols.'

The historical point is correct: Muslims and Hindus *have* lived, for long periods, at peace with each other in India. Furthermore, as we have already seen, some ulama have declared that the Vedas (Hindu Scripture) are indeed revealed from God, and that consequently Hindus count as People of the Book:

'What happened in the past is that Muslims treated Hindus as the People of the Book. They simply made the ruling – I think probably to facilitate the rule of those areas. However, it does seem clear that they are much closer to polytheism, to being what we call *mushrikun*, and that is something we absolutely cannot accept in Islam.'

JB: 'But if you cannot accept it, what should you do supposing you are in a majority in some country where Hindus are living?'

'Here we're on sticky ground. I don't think I can really answer that. I am not answering, not because I think we would have to kill them all, but there must be some way that it would be dealt with. There would have to be some sort of treaty – it would be a treaty like those we made when we were ruling India, whereby they live in their way and pay tax to live within the Muslim state. But I don't know how free they would be to practise their religion, or what efforts there would be to convert them or to rectify their belief, in a way which would be acceptable to us. It's not an attack on the individual, on the harm he is doing in believing something wrong, and it's not because we are intolerant of one person believing whatever he wants; it is because the net effect is that they are establishing a faith or a belief which is erroneous and which is leading people astray. It is our duty as Muslims at least to set a limit to what people are saying adversely about our Creator.'

But even here, the Muslim voice is not unanimous. It may well be that realistic pragmatism led Muslim rulers to decide that Hindus counted as People of the Book — not only in order to facilitate government, but even more because it allowed intermarriage: Muslim men can marry women who are in that category. But having made that recognition, and having come to know Hinduism better, it is entirely possible for Muslims to recognize the truth of the Hindu position, that they are not worshipping idols at all. The signpost is not to be confused with what it points to:

'In Islamic history, we have seen Muslims being very creative in their relationship with Hindus. When the Muslims first entered India, several hundred years ago, the issue of idolatry confronted Muslims immediately. From what they could see, people were worshipping sculpture in temples, which for the Muslims would be idol worship; and that in Islam is *kufr* or unbelief; or *shirk*, the worship of several gods, whereas Islam is very much a monotheistic faith. But then Muslims went beyond appearance to examine what Hindus were really involved in — that Hindus saw these images in fact as different manifestations of the one Being. In that case, it fell within the Islamic framework, and as a result, Muslims were able to interact creatively with Hindus, to the extent that Muslims married Hindus, when the Qur'ān says specifically that you cannot marry an idol-worshipper. So, using the tools of the faith creatively, Muslims were able to overcome this dilemma. That does not mean to say that they were necessarily right. Maybe today

Muslims would take a different view on this. But always, now and in the future, there will be reinterpretation, which results in different attitudes to the variety of faiths.'

Making all this as general as possible, the Muslim attitude to non-Muslim religions is that non-Muslims are capable of the worship of God and of the reward that will result from this on the Day of Judgement; and their works of service in the world and to their neighbours will be equally rewarded. Where non-Muslims are living in this way, they should not be disturbed:

'Any place where the name of God is remembered and adored is a *masjid*. The word *masjid*, therefore, is a universal term. It does not apply only to a place where Muslims perform their worship. A temple, a church, a synagogue, where the name of God is being adored and remembered, is just as much a *masjid* as a mosque is for Muslims.'

The Penalty for Apostasy from Islam

Does it follow, from all that, that it is then a matter of indifference if a Muslim ceases to be a Muslim and begins to worship God in another religion; or indeed if he or she ceases to recognize God at all and becomes an atheist? The impression of Islam is that if a Muslim converts to another religion, the penalty for that apostasy is death. But once again, the reality is more complex and more fragile, because the penalty is not specified in the Qur'ān:

'Muslim law says that a person may not apostatize Islam. This really comes from the Tradition, not from the Qur'ān at all. The Qur'ān puts the punishment for apostasy in the hereafter, not in this world [see ii. 117/114]. There is no legislation in the Qur'ān about apostasy to the effect that it should be punished by capital punishment. There is a Hadith or Tradition from the

Prophet, "Whosoever changes his religion should be excluded", but that was not looked upon by many scholars as mandatory. For instance, Abu Hanifa, who is one of the great scholars of Islam, thought that if a woman changed her religion, she may be left alone – perhaps advised every day to come back to Islam, but she is left alone. In other words, the sentence is there, but it is not applied until she dies. And when asked why this should be, when the word is "whosoever", which includes a woman, the answer is that the woman is not a political danger. That means that apostasy would only become a crime if it were combined with an attempt to take the state and subvert Islam altogether. A contemporary of Abu Hanifa, al-Awzayy, who belonged to a different and more traditional school, the school that follows the text, said that both men and women should be given the same privilege: in other words, if there is no plot to take over the state, no plot for a *coup d'état*, both men and women should be allowed an indefinite period to recant. In my view, we cannot apply the penalty in the modern world, particularly in a country like Britain. We are not in a majority. In any case, a person who apostatizes has put himself or herself outside the Muslim law. She or he has the freedom guaranteed by the law of the country in which she or he resides. In a Muslim country, let me say that very, very seldom do you see or hear of someone being executed – in modern times – for apostasy. In Egypt, for example, Neguib Mahfouz wrote a book which was regarded as very much against Islam. All that the authorities have done there is to ban the book, and to stop it from being published officially. Unofficially, it is sold all over Cairo and elsewhere. The basic point in Islam is that you cannot compel anyone. One of the last verses revealed to the Prophet states, "There is no compulsion in religion."'

Here, of course, we are getting close to Salman Rushdie and *The Satanic Verses*. Mahfouz is an Egyptian novelist, a winner of the Nobel Prize for literature, whose questioning of Islam in *Children of Gebalawi* is far more searching than that of Rushdie. He has faced opposition and at least one physical attack, and some individual claims that he should be executed. But there has been no fatwa issued against him. The difference is clear: a Muslim can raise sceptical questions; whether it becomes a communal issue depends very much on the way in which he does so:

'In Rushdie's case, the issue revolves around what I would call reverent scepticism and irreverent scepticism. There are many reverent sceptics in Islam. We have a tradition of that. Of course there are tussles with orthodoxy, as there are in all religious traditions. The issue is the irreverent scepticism. It's one thing for the content of scepticism to be iconoclastic, it's quite another for it to be gratuitously provocative. He has done himself a disservice. He could have raised those same points without this kind of language or without taking an actual event, such as the Satanic verses [historically these were verses whispered by Satan to Muhammad, mimicking Qur'ān, which were subsequently recognized by him for what they were and denounced], and making it the basis for sweeping generalization and gratuitous remarks. Neguib Mahfouz's book is a piece of reverent scepticism, and I respect that. Religions ought to allow that kind of critique, since otherwise they become completely outdated. But Rushdie does not set any agenda for the Muslim enlightenment; after all, what *are* the issues he is raising? The real point is that Salman Rushdie is not a conscientious atheist, he is just an atheist. There's a big difference between conscientious atheism and fashionable atheism which flirts with certain attitudes in the West.'

So at least theoretically a Muslim should be free to change his or her religion (so long as it does not threaten the state) and to criticize Islam while he or she remains a Muslim (so long as it is a critique which remains reverent). It is only if they turn on Islam and attack it aggressively that the penalty of death may come into question – but even then it is a highly disputed matter:

'From the time of the Prophet, that penalty was there. But there has been a lot of controversy about that among the theologians and jurists. The first instance that I have got in the Hadith concerns Moadh ibn Jabal, who was one of the Companions of the Prophet. He was sent by the Prophet to Yemen, to be its governor. When he went there he found one man tied to a tree. He said, "Why have you done this to this man?" He was told, "First he was a Jew, then he became a Muslim. Now he is slandering Islam, and he is no longer a Muslim." He said, "Don't you know the punishment for it?" And he drew his sword and beheaded him. So from that the jurists drew the conclusion that the penalty for apostasy is death. In later juridical literature, we find that there have been certain developments regarding this, but the general consensus about this particular penalty is that if you become a Muslim, then give up Islam, then the penalty for you is death. But if you are a non-Muslim or an atheist even, then *lakum dinka wa li adDin*: to you your religion and to me mine.'

But clearly even that general consensus can be challenged, given the relative insecurity of its foundation:

'There is an area of difference here. It has been claimed that the Prophet has said that if a man changes his religion, then kill him. The complete Hadith is: "If a man changes his religion and acts against the Muslims, then kill him." So if a man changes his religion and acts aggressively against the Muslims, you should treat him in the same way that you would a non-Muslim who acts aggressively against Islam: defend yourself, in other words. Some scholars have taken that to say that apostasy itself must be punished by death. Some other scholars – and many of them are eminent scholars – said, no, in the case of an apostate you just advise him, and you keep advising him throughout his life. So there is no unanimity about that at all. I have to tell you that for myself, I accept every single verse of the Qur'ān automatically, and I have no quarrel with any verse, and I read the Qur'ān very critically, by the way. But with Hadith, or with many of them, it is different, because we cannot always be sure that it is a saying of the Prophet. It comes to us from Mr A who heard it from Mr B who heard it from Mr C who heard that the Prophet said it. Through this chain doubt must arise, and testing these Traditions is a scholarly thing that has gone on through the ages. So when I hear a Hadith, I have to go back to the Qur'ān and say, "Does it agree with the Qur'ān?", and if it does I accept it. If it does not, then I must refuse it. Who said that? The Prophet himself. So if I go back to the Qur'ān with the question of apostasy, I find that one of the very latest or last of the verses to be revealed in the Qur'ān says, "Let there be no compulsion in religion"; so what right can anyone have now to say that no one has the right to apostatize? Of course the right to apostasy is there. The judgement of that belongs only to God. If an apostate behaves in a good and just manner, let him be treated justly, and with mercy as well. If he is aggressive, then you have to deal with him in a way to stop his aggressiveness. If you take the Hadith itself, it's narrated by one man only, and the Hadith that is narrated by one man is not as strong as those that are narrated by more. It is certainly weaker.'

Even so the possibility of the death penalty remains if it is combined with an attack on Islam, because then it is moving into the domain of treason:

'Since there is no compulsion in Islam, a person is free to change his religion, but one might then come to a point where he has become a traitor. A person is free to change, but he cannot then insult and abuse people. There is a clear-cut difference in that.'

The penalty, therefore, is for treason, not really for apostasy, though the two may simply be equated, and then the difference is not so clear-cut:

'Apostasy is an act of treason against Islam. What most of the scholars say is that if a person leaves Islam, and does nothing actively to hurt Islam, that's fine. But if he tries actively to hurt Islam, as Rushdie has done, then we must put a stop to it, even if it means killing him.'

If the real offence is treason, then it becomes a question how one can be a traitor of that active kind if (as we have heard repeatedly) there is no Islamic state in existence. But there is always the metaphorical community, the umma, which transcends the nation-state, and whose realization in practice is the Muslim vision and horizon. At this level, religion and ideology coincide:

'Any person who leaves the House of Islam and then actively pursues an ideological enmity towards Islam, his action would be defined as treason in Islamic law. There is no distinction between religious and political authority in Islam, so that treason and apostasy aggravated by enmity are the same crime. Treason may be a secular term, but in Islam you cannot make that distinction. The Qur'ān has no such resources. That does not prevent human ingenuity from having invented them afterwards.'

The Satanic Verses

It is in this context that the reaction to Rushdie's novel has to be understood. Clearly, it was not a simple matter of blasphemy – if it was that at all:

'As far as blasphemy is concerned, there is no equivalent word for that in Arabic in the first place [the nearest equivalent is *sabb*: see ix. 74 of *kufr*], so it can hardly be a punishable offence. In fact the Christians are accused of having what you might call blasphemed against God, by calling Jesus the Son of God, but no penalty was prescribed for them. It would in any case be unworkable, because it would apply to a whole community. Rushdie is not accused of either apostasy or blasphemy by the Muslim jurists. He is accused of *fasad*, public disorder. That is a Qur'ānic term in sura 5. He is also accused, under a very obscure law, of being a *shatin*. A *shatin* is a man who insults a messenger of God – any messenger of God. It does not have to be Muhammad, because Islam recognizes all messengers of God, including Moses and Jesus. So anyone who insults a messenger of God becomes a *shatin*. The peculiarity of the *shatin* punishment, as opposed to the punishment for *fasad*, is that the *fasad* punishment can be revoked: if you express repentance, you can be forgiven. In the case of the other, it is irrevocable. You cannot ask for forgiveness, you cannot be forgiven.'

It is clear, therefore, that although the issue is advertised in the media as blasphemy, that is not the Muslim concern – it has only become so indirectly, because the limitations of the existing laws in the UK relating to blasphemy have been exposed. The issues, for Muslims, are much wider:

The Muslims have never said that the Prophet was a divine person [so to insult the Prophet cannot be a matter of blasphemy]. All Muslims hold the Prophet as a human being. But Muslim scholars and non-Muslim scholars alike have attested to the fact that he was a good person, no matter what they may hold him to be ultimately. In *The Satanic Verses* we find that the Prophet's life has been turned upside down: a good man has been made a bad man, and his family has been described in a derogatory way. No human being, whether living or dead, should be addressed in the foul language of the kind that he has used. Language is very important in ethics, and Muslims feel that the manner in which he has used language is unacceptable. The Prophet Muhammad was a religious person, the Muslim community is a religious community, and ethics play an important part. The honour, dignity and nobility of the living and the dead are guarded in Islam by a strict procedure of etiquette. Even if a person was a murderer in this world, once that person dies, that criminality dies with him. We are only allowed to speak of whatever good that person did. If we feel that he did not do any good, then we must be silent. In this case, we are talking about a very important person in Islam. The honour and dignity which we accord to the living we must accord also to the dead. That is the essence of what Muslims are concerned with, although unfortunately, this has hardly been understood.'

JB: 'But should the defence of the Prophet mean the execution of the offender?'

'No, of course not, because this is not new for Muslims. The Prophet has been attacked throughout history [cf. Prideaux in chapter 1], and even in his lifetime he was attacked in a more disparaging way than we find today. But people who proceed down that road must accept the responsibility for the upset which they know that they are going to cause, and Mr Rushdie certainly knew the upset he would cause in the Muslim community. He is an educated person, he comes from a Muslim background, and he knows the Muslim ethos, therefore he knew that this would cause offence. In the use of our freedom (and Islam would like all our freedoms to be protected), freedom must be exercised with wisdom and with responsibility, so that peace can be maintained. This is the ideal in Islam, that there may be *salam*, peace, and freedoms cannot be allowed to be used – or misused – in such a way that peace is disrupted.'

So the issue is not one of 'freedom of speech' in the abstract, although that is how many Western critics have taken it. Freedoms, including freedom of speech, are always and everywhere limited by the bounds of decency – bounds which, by Muslim standards, have clearly been exceeded in the case of this novel:

'Freedom of speech is not the issue at all. Freedom of speech is already restricted under the law, for example in countless enactments to do with sedition, to do with contempt of court, defamation of character, libel and so on. No democracy is absolute in these freedoms. The question is about its limits. It so happens that Muslims as a group are not protected under the law in this country – naturally, because this is not historically a Muslim country. But it is a case of double standards if, when it comes to outraging Muslim sensibilities, people appeal to freedom of speech in defence, while all the time there are many other things not allowed – racist writings, for example, are routinely censored, other writings are thought to be obscene, and so on. So this freedom is obviously being practised in a selective way. It does not lead to an outlawing of critique or debate if there is a proper recognition of Muslim sensibilities. I don't deny that there are many other factors involved – there may be issues of insecurity in relatively poor immigrant communities, there may be external funding and so on. But I think at the end of the day, if we are going to have some limits to cynicism in this affair, we have to recognize that some people are authentic in their outrage. The degree of outrage and the fact that it refuses to die down is an indication that it is authentic. For after all, it is politically inexpedient for Muslims to continue to protest in the way that they are, because it is likely to lead to serious consequences for them. But I think they see it as a matter of principle. I know I can only speak for myself, because it is hard to judge in affairs of the heart, but I know for myself that I am campaigning because I see it as a matter of principle. Believe me, there are no foreign sponsors here — you can look at the state of my house to know that there is no foreign funding here!'

JB: 'What *is* the principle for which you are campaigning?'

'The principle is that while it is right and proper for people to take reverent and conscientious exception to a particular traditional faith, including people who are born in it, it is not right and proper for people gratuitously to insult the sanctities and sensibilities of a major world constituency of this kind. Islam is not a sect. It is a major world Faith of genius and vitality, and it is a prejudice to deny that it produces men of character. So I think that for Rushdie to treat and portray Muhammad in the way he has is utterly indefensible, because I do not believe that any moral or religious tradition of this kind of fecundity and antiquity has ever been created by men who were wicked, which is the message of his book. Remember that he is saying that Mahound, or Muhammad, is irredeemably evil. He is not saying that he had some evil tendencies, or that he had some tendency to temptation. Muslims can easily accept that, because, unlike Christ, Muhammad was only human. But to say that a man who founded a major world religion was irredeemably evil is, I think, utterly indefensible, and it cannot be tolerated in a civilized society.'

JB: 'For what, then, are you campaigning?'

'That the book should be voluntarily withdrawn, or, if that fails, that perhaps there should be some enactment to compel withdrawal, or at least that a law should be made which would make any publication like this impossible in the future.'

109

So no Muslims doubt the deep offence of the publication of the novel. They may disagree about what should be done. They may think, for example, that the Ayatollah's fatwa was too strong a response:

'Where you find Muslims not waiting to talk and discuss with people their errors, but instead killing them, in general I think that is deeply unIslamic. I think the fatwa that was pronounced by Imam Khomeini against Salman Rushdie was incorrect, in that, if the man had committed blasphemy, he should be tried. He has the right to answer, he also has the right to repent [but that, as we have seen, depends on the offence], but no one can pronounce death on him. There is no lynch law in Islam, nor authoritarian, military type of executions. There are due processes of law to be followed. In the case of blasphemy/apostasy, where people say things which I find unacceptable, I understand the historical basis of the punishment for this so-called crime (and I call it "so-called"): Islam implies the creation of a perfect Islamic state, so the idea of apostasy is very closely linked with that of treason. However, the idea of execution for blasphemy is not in the Qur'ān. That was a later development – I think it was developed by ibn Taymir (but I am not a scholar and I may be wrong) because of the pressures on the Islamic umma from the outside, from the Mongols. Personally I think it is unIslamic. I think you are obliged to listen to your antagonist, and to those who disagree with you, with courtesy, and to talk to them and to persuade them. The whole lynching mentality is one of fear. Intolerance is born of fear, not just of the other, but of the other inside oneself.'

Or again, they may think that the reaction in the UK was a great missed opportunity to show how Islam transcends and deals with offence:

'We have to view the Salman Rushdie issue as that of a man

who is deliberately insulting God and the Prophet and the Muslims and everyone else, me included. But then we have to go back to the Qur'ān and see what the Qur'ān says about that. Verse 140 in the sura *an-Nisaa*, which is sura number 4, says this: If you hear some from the unbelievers, or the hypocrites, insulting God or the word of God, then do not sit with them until they talk about something else. That is all. In other words, when I am sitting with Salman Rushdie, or I am sitting with his book, and I hear or read what he says, I should say, "Well, listen, if you are going to talk like this, I am not going to sit here and take all this. I am going to go away, and if you are going to change the subject and talk about something sensible, I will then come back and sit with you." That is the Qur'ānic way, the gentle way, the merciful way, the effective way, of dealing with something like that, not the way that we have seen lately, with death threats – not even with the banning of it, because the Qur'ān is not a Book that goes in for banning other books. In fact the Qur'ān does the opposite: it gives an airing to all the ridiculous ideas that some of the unbelievers have held. So it is not a banning Book, it is not a burning Book, and it is certainly not a death-threatening, capital punishment Book at all. That is what the Qur'ān says, verse 140, sura 4; anybody can read it, anybody can compare that with what we have seen lately, and can see the very big and sharp contrast between the two.'

But all Muslims agree that a serious offence was committed. When the Ayatollah formalized that judgement in the fatwa, he was not alone in that judgement. Once the warrant and argument for the fatwa has been made clear and has been agreed, whether it comes from a Sunni or Shia source, and while it may still be contested if there are grounds for doing so, it has authority and cannot be cancelled. That point has already been made in a general way (pp. 26f); applying it now to the specific case:

'You ask specifically about the fatwa with regard to Salman Rushdie: Mr Khomeini has not been the only one to issue such a fatwa. When the Muslim states met in Riyadh, they issued a very similar fatwa, simply worded differently. The rule of Islam is very well known, that in the context of an Islamic state, anyone who is guilty of undermining the very foundation of that state is guilty of high treason, and he is to be punished by death. The problem here arises because the act has been committed by someone living in a non-Muslim state, where people are subject to different laws (and it is a fundamental principle of Islam that Muslims in such circumstances must abide by the laws of the country they are in). But the fatwa as such cannot be renounced by any person, just as you could not ask the Pope to renounce any of the Ten Commandments, or the Chief Rabbi to renounce anything that is written in the Torah or the Talmud. I should have expected the British government in these circumstances to use a little bit more common sense, and not throw its whole weight behind one author who has been paid to insult a large, large community in this country and across the world. Yet they chose to promote and protect him in the name of freedom of speech, disregarding the fact that he also had very insulting remarks in his book against the Prime Minister, using four-letter words, and nasty remarks about the Queen, where he implied some sort of sexual scandal involving her. Yet the government threw its whole weight behind him as though to teach the Muslim community of this country a lesson, to the effect that if you think, now that you are an integrated part of this country, you can have your own views, forget about that.'

For those Muslims who believe that something stronger should be done than simply discussing the matter with the offender, and given that they are subject to UK law, what can they hope or expect to do?

'We certainly cannot administer the death penalty to Salman Rushdie here in England, because the British government has made a treaty with us, and we would have to request that he be sent to a Muslim country. We should state quite clearly that the judgement is correct. But we cannot apply it in a non-Muslim country.'

JB: 'So you are saying that he ought to be extradited in order to be executed?'

'We should ask that he be extradited. If we have a treaty, surely that should be respected.'

JB: 'But extradited in order to be executed?'

'Well, in the same way that in America treason still carries the death penalty, so does treason carry the death penalty in Islam. Treason and blasphemy are the same thing in Islam.'

It is on this basis that General Zia-ul-Haq enacted the law in Pakistan requiring the death penalty for blasphemy – i.e., for defamation of God or of His Prophet. The use of that law as an instrument of persecution against other religious minorities is yet another of those issues where there is (or should be) a Muslim protest against the abuse of Islam.

The Status of the Bahā'īs and the Ahmadīyya

It is this transcendent sense of umma, against which Mr Rushdie has offended in terms of treachery, which explains the different Muslim treatment of the two religious communities, the Bahā'ī and the Ahmadīyya. Given the basic point about no compulsion in religion, these two religious movements ought presumably to have freedom to live in their own way in Muslim countries. But both, and particularly the Ahmadīyya, have experienced persecution in some Muslim countries. Both of them came into being in the nineteenth century, and both of them are rooted in Islam, but they are of a very different kind. The Bahā'īs recognize a series of Manifestations of God (*mazāhir-i ilāhī*), who reveal the divine purpose for humanity. These include Muhammad, and culminate (for the present age) in Bahā'u'llāh of the nineteenth century. For a Muslim, this may seem to call in question the claim that Muhammad is 'the seal [i.e. last] of the Prophets'. The Ahmadīyya claim to be derived from one who completes the prophetic line, and they therefore seem to other Muslims to be denying the finality and completeness of the Qur'ān. The Muslim evaluation of them will therefore turn on whether they are perceived as new religious movements (in which case they would be regarded as being in error but not as threatening, unless politically they were threatening the state), or whether they are perceived as an attack on Islam (in which case a war in defence of Islam is allowed and indeed encouraged):

They are not Muslims, full stop. The Ahmadīyya and the Bahā'īs are not Muslims. So the difference is that if a Christian comes along and says, "This is what I believe," we would help him to be a good Christian in our countries. If an Ahmadīyya comes along and says, "I am a good Muslim," we have got to stop it, because it is not Islam. He is insulting and mocking Islam, and that has to be stopped.'

There would then be exactly the same issue of what form the 'stopping' should take, as in Salman Rushdie's case. The definition of their relation to Islam becomes critical:

'Interpretations of Islam are all permitted, within certain limits, that is, within the limits of the Qur'ānic text. Every religion has to have boundaries, and in our case the boundaries are the text. If interpretation goes beyond the textual possibilities, then we just cannot accept it. If it is a possible meaning of the text, it must be allowed, as a statement made by al-Ghazālī [the great medieval scholar who has a status roughly comparable to that of Aquinas in Christianity or of Maimonides in Judaism] affirms that if a statement is made by a Muslim, and it has ninety-nine possibilities out of a hundred of being heretical or of indicating unbelief, and one possibility of being able to be brought within the boundaries of belief, then you must accept it and give it legitimacy. In other words, we do not expel people for just the slightest deviation. But if it is a gross deviation, going beyond the limits of the text, and beyond the limits of what our concept of Islam is, then it is not possible to accept that interpretation as being within Islam.

'People can claim that they are a new religion. I think that the Bahā'īs do exactly that quite openly. They do not say that they are Muslims. They say that they are a new religion. With the Ahmadīyya, it is a different matter, because they say that they are still Muslims. They claim to remain Muslims. As you know, they are divided into two: one section says that the founder was simply a reformer, a *mujadid*, a revivalist; the others believe him to be a prophet, and that is probably the main body of the movement. But the Muslims in general believe that there is no prophet after the Prophet, and therefore they reject that side of the movement altogether. As for the first group, who claim that he was only a revivalist, Muslims suspect that they are simply the Trojan horse of the other group, and they are worried about it.

'As you probably know, the Ahmadīyya were tolerated for a very long time. There were no restrictions on them. It is only since I think 1974 that, under the late 'Alī Bhutto, the Pakistani parliament declared them to be a separate religion, and consequently the whole Muslim world took the same attitude, since the movement had begun in Pakistan. So far as the Bahā'īs are concerned, it is not a religious matter. In my view, as a minority in Iran, they were exploited by the Shah and by the regime, and many of them joined the Savak and were very prominent in the Shah's oppressive administration. This unfortunately is often the lot of minorities under dictatorships, and the fall of the Shah meant that they would be punished. But I do not think that the Bahā'īs *per se* are being persecuted in Iran.'

JB: 'But if there *were* to be any pressure against *all* the Bahā'īs as a community – difficulty in getting jobs, for example – that would be contrary to Islam?'

'Oh yes, certainly. I don't see any reason for that at all. These people were not Muslims who have apostatized, they were born in that particular Faith. They have to be treated like *dhimmis*, protected people within the society. They should be given all the rights accorded to them.'

However, the belief that the Bahā'īs have not been persecuted in Iran has been contradicted repeatedly and in detail. Here is yet another test case for the world community of Islam: given all that has been said in this book about the positive toleration (and endorsement) of religious minorities, how can this be made a living fact today? And how can it be made a fact of such manifest truth that it contradicts the fears expressed by the outsiders at the opening of this book? This is a challenge deeply felt by all the contributors to this book, and one to which we will return at the end.

The Nature of Human Nature

Here, as in every other matter, the basic 'parameters' or 'boundaries' are set by the Qur'ān. This is absolute and non-negotiable. But it does not follow from that, that Islam is fixed or frozen in the sixth century. Islam and Sharia are open to continuing debate and interpretation – and much of this chapter has seen exactly that process in action. Nevertheless, because of the content of the Qur'ān, there are some things which are, so to speak, frozen – they cannot be changed. Among these are the basic constituents of human nature, summarized in the term *fitra*. That nature is created by God, and the Qur'ān is related to it by offering the guidance that will lead it to Paradise and reward after death. That is why there is, in Islam, not literalism, but a conservative respect in relation to the text:

'I don't feel that God's creation changes in its intrinsic nature. We go through stages of development, but I don't believe that there is a fundamental change in our nature. The Qur'ān says that we are created with a *fitra*, which is a basic nature, which, we presume from the verse in the Qur'ān, is inclined towards goodness.'

It follows, in relation to that fixed and given human nature, that the Qur'ān offers guidance which must apply to every generation, no matter what the cultural variations or the technological advances may be:

'Human beings have not changed so much since Adam and Eve. We are fundamentally exactly the same as them. So the Qur'ān and the Sunna remain applicable for all times. Today we have got the cars and the aeroplanes and space rockets. We are not saying, "Get rid of those and go back to camels." That is silly. This world was given to us almost as a gift by God. There is so much in it, and God says, "Use it; but use it in a good way to serve other people, and be obedient." Islam is not asking you to be something else. It is asking you to be yourself, a human being, and not an animal; to live like a human being, not like a dog on the street.'

But this idea of *fitra*, or of a fixed nature, is another point at which the outsider becomes alarmed, for two reasons. One is that the whole issue of a fixed human nature has been called in question by the exploration, particularly in anthropology, of cultural relativity, since it follows from the recognition of extreme cultural diversity that the idea of 'human nature' may itself be a cultural construction. The other has more immediate and practical relevance: does it mean that the nature of men and of women is immutably fixed in the Qur'ān in such a way that women will always and necessarily be subordinate to men? Or is that in itself a wrong understanding of the way in which Islam sees the relationship between men and women?

CHAPTER FOUR

THE NATURE OF WOMEN AND THEIR STATUS

Women and Men

Fitra implies that human nature as it should be is created by God in a way that is fixed and invariant (see glossary). But human nature is not itself undifferentiated. It is divided into the two sexes. But that means that the differences are themselves important and fixed in creation:

'Men and women were both created by God, and both men and women are good things in creation. We should live together in harmony, because men and women are two partners who make up the whole. So if a man is on his own, he is only half what he should be, and the same for a woman. Since God created us, he knows us better than we know ourselves. Men and women were created different, and they will never be the same. Each and every one of our cells is implanted with this difference. Every cell of mine is that of a woman. So we are very different, and our roles are very different. Therefore, because of their differences in physique and mental capabilities, et cetera, their roles are very different: a woman is much more sensitive than a man.'

JB: 'Are these differences in sensitivity acquired culturally, or are women born with them?'

'We are born with them. A boy and a girl are completely different.'

The precise map of what the natural distinctions are may be disputed, but not the basic observation of differences in nature which are fixed by birth and lead to different roles:

There are certain aspects of human nature which men and women share in common. There is no difference, for example, in intellect or things like that. The real difference is in the emotions, and in certain aspects of character. There are certain things which are largely masculine traits, and others which are largely feminine. With males, there is this leaning towards a rash way of behaving, very easily led and very quickly aroused – and not just sexually, but in anger and other emotions; whereas a woman has more of an inner patience, and that shows, I think, in childbirth – something that men would never be let by God to go through; I think He has realized that we are not capable of coping with that. I know I am making light of it, but I think these are things which are inbred into our characters.'

But this leads us at once to one of the major items in the outsider's negative impression of Islam. The extremely recent experience of women in taking control over their own lives and bodies has called into question the belief that there is an invariant feminine nature; perhaps the idea and the definition of nature are themselves cultural creations. That possibility then reinforces the outsider's suspicion that Islam is threatening to women, precisely because it does fix their nature in a way that makes them for ever subordinate to men. But is that a true perception or account?

The Role of Women

The immediate Muslim answer is to say that Islam had already anticipated and established from the start what the twentieth century has belatedly been discovering for itself. It was Islam which first insisted that women were indeed different but nevertheless equal. From the earliest days, women have been prominent in the history of Islam – especially Aisha, the favourite among Muhammad's wives:

'If you look at the role of women in the earliest days of Islam, such as that of his young wife Aisha, she is credited with having transmitted to us one third of our religion – that is, mostly Traditions about the family life of the Prophet. When she was asked what the Prophet did at home, she said that he helped his wife. That meant that he swept the floor, he mended his clothes and his sandals. I also think that it is a highly significant fact that, although motherhood is highly respected in Islam (thus when the Prophet was asked, "Whom should I honour most?", he said three times, "Your mother," and only after that he said, "Your father"), Aisha, one of the most highly venerated women in the Muslim body of tradition, was not a mother. She was a young girl whom the Prophet advised his Companions to consult on religious matters in his absence. She was also the executor of her father's will. Her father, Abu Bakr, became the first of the rightly guided Caliphs. When he died she was the one entrusted with the execution of his will, not her brother, Abd ur-Rahman. So I think that in the person of Aisha, and also in that of his first wife Khadija (who was Muhammad's first employer and who owned her own business), we have an example, as Muslim women, of a woman acting independently in the public sphere, with great authority and with great dignity; and yet they are also models of women in a more traditional role with a husband.'

Coming down to the present day, it is simply a matter of fact that women in Muslim countries can achieve high positions in many careers; and this may be true even when in other respects – say, in dress – they may appear to be in a traditional role:

'Muslim women have different appearances in different cultures. Not all Muslim women dress in great black robes with veils. They do, perhaps, in Saudi Arabia, in their public personae, but these women who are dressed in black veils are nevertheless doctors, lawyers, teachers and broadcasters, so the style of dress does not necessarily limit them. I would also like to say that women in Saudi Arabia, although they are about the most extreme example of modern segregated women, are among the wealthiest women in the world. Because of Muslim laws of inheritance, women inherit independently; they have complete control in law over their property, and no other person has any right to interfere in law, so that in Saudi Arabia there are banks that service women only; and as far as I understand it, women own about one third of the property in Saudi Arabia. Throughout Muslim history women have been judges, and as you may know, in the constitution of Pakistan women are included as possible heads of state, as Benazir Bhutto at present demonstrates. That constitution was drawn up by Muslim scholars, and although it was disputed by some, that is because Muslim scholars do not, and are not required to, concur on every matter.'

Despite the truth of all that, the impression or appearance to the outsider – no doubt based in part on ignorance – is clearly very different. That is partly because the physical appearance of some Muslim women is as it was described above. But the heavy veiling is not itself required. It is a cultural extension of the requirement of basic decency in clothing, and the *hijab*, usually translated as 'veil', belongs to that requirement.

The 'Veil'

So what exactly is the 'veil'?

The *hijab* means literally "a barrier". However, legally it is used to refer to the scarf worn by a woman, or in a wider sense it can refer to the full dress worn by a man or a woman, as required by Muslim law.'

The idea of 'the barrier' is one of the most fundamental in Islamic ethics of daily life, and one which, as we will see, is of great importance in Muslim education. Many of the detailed rules of behaviour or of deportment are to prevent sin or temptation even coming over the threshold. In the case of clothing and the *hijab*, it is to prevent arousal by sexual temptation.

But in that case, why is the barrier of clothing not required equally for men? The immediate answer is that it is – men do have rules of decency in dress:

'Muslim law dictates that neither men nor women should wear provocative clothing. Unfortunately, like everything else, the ones with power interpret the law to suit themselves. So many men have used the provisions about clothing to oppress women, and to allow themselves freedom. But the reality is that both men and women, according to Muslim law, should not wear clothing to be provocative to one another. They should regard each other as persons, not as sex objects.'

JB: 'Is the veil necessary in Islam?'

'Not at all, not at all. In fact at the present time, in one of the most conservative papers in Egypt, *AnNur*, a series of about twenty-one articles is being published in which the writer says that the veil is prohibited in Islam. He argues from the point of view of the most fundamental aspects of Muslim law itself and from the statements of the Prophet. So really the veil is not at all mandatory, by any means.'

Despite popular impressions to the contrary, the *hijab* does not mean that women have to cover themselves in an all-over veil, with only their eyes showing:

'Women do not have to cover their faces. If anyone was to

say that, it would be a mistake. The usual limit, which is set out in the Hadith, and is accepted by the four schools (though with some differences: the Hanbali and the Shafii schools, for example, prefer a further covering, but that is not obligatory) is that the face and hands of the women are allowed to be left uncovered, whereas the rest of her should be covered. Basically that comes down to a scarf headcovering. In itself it is acceptable to have different practices, but when those practices assume the importance of the religion itself and are justified as part of our religion, that's when ignorance has gone so deep that people just don't recognize what is culture and custom, and what is religion.'

Indeed, for one Muslim woman, excessive veiling has exactly the opposite of the intended effect:

'With the concepts of decency and modesty, what is considered to be decent in one society is not considered to be so in another. Modesty is a social construct. It's a matter of interpretation. What I find most objectionable about the idea of veiling myself completely – although if I lived in Saudi Arabia I would have no hesitation in doing that – is that it makes what I consider to be public parts of myself private, and perhaps even to be eroticized, and I find that, as a human being, to be unacceptable.'

The Authority of Men

Once again, we can recognize the plea that for Islam to be itself, it must move, not forward into further cultural accretion, but back – back to Sharia. But in that case, how do the Qur'ān and Hadith, which together create the patterns of life which are formalized in Sharia, envisage the status of men and women in relation to each other? Certainly as equal, albeit with different roles and responsibilities. They require each, as we have already heard, to become fully themselves. In marriage, men and women are to be a garment to each other.

Nevertheless, within that partnership, the man is the senior partner. The Qur'ān says that he has a rank or degree (*darajah*) over his wife: 'Women have rights over them (like those of men) of an honourable kind, but men have *darajah* over them' (ii. 228). In another verse, it is said that men are *qawwumun* over women: 'Because God has given pre-eminence over the other, and because they support them from their means . . . As to those women whom you suspect of ill-conduct, admonish them, banish them to their beds, beat them. If they obey you, do not seek any further way against them' (iv. 34/38). It is clearly a matter of interpretation what the Arabic words mean. But given that they imply *some* distinction, what is involved in practice?

'Islam says that although men and women have the same rights and the same duties in terms of human relations and in the family, the men have a rank over them. That rank is really a matter of – shall we say – chairmanship of the family. The family is a social organization, and Islam cares enormously for the family, because it regards the family as the basic unit of society. Now you have to organize it. You have to have certain rules and regulations. These rules and regulations will be followed or enforced only in times of dispute. If there is an agreement between husband and wife on anything at all, it's left to them. Between husband and wife nobody interferes. If the wife is the leader and the decision maker of the family, nobody interferes. But if there is a dispute between them and this creates a problem for them, then we say, "Well, look, a rule of thumb: the husband is the boss in the family." But his position is based on real consultation and agreement within his family. So the rank that he takes is more like the position of a chairman than the position of a dictator. Then in the case of the other verse, with the word *qawwumun*: "men are standing over women": this term is very ambiguous, and it has had a lot of interpretations. One interpretation was made by one of our scholars who died only about two years ago and he said, "It means that they are servants of the women." They are standing like waiters or attendants on women. They are in that position of waiting on the women because under Muslim law a man is obliged to maintain his wife, in all aspects – clothe her, feed her, house her. That's his responsibility, regardless of how wealthy she herself is; she might even be wealthier than he is. Nonetheless, under Muslim law that is his position. And because he does have that obligation, that is why he becomes the chairman of the family, because all the decisions about housing, clothing, finance will be his responsibility.'

The roles, therefore, go back to obligations in the Qur'ān. As always in Islam, there should be no need for the exercise of that authority if the appropriate conversation has already taken place. But human nature being what it is, there is no doubt where the final locus of authority is:

'It is the difference between men and women. Even inside the home, where the Prophet said that the woman is the queen of the house, ultimately if there is a decision to be made and it requires one vote, as it were, it will have to be the man's, because the man will always be dominant. That's the way men are: they are more aggressive and dominant.'

But still the fact remains that while the Qur'ān as the basic constraint on Muslim life is absolute and non-negotiable, its meanings are not – that is to say, the exegesis of the Qur'ān is always open and continuing, provided that it falls within the bounds of the textually possible. Thus in the case of those verses, a quite different interpretation is possible, relating them to the relationship of the family to the outside world:

'In my view the verse means, "Men shall have full care of women". Men's role in the family is as leaders of the family *vis-à-vis* the outside world. In other words, they represent the family to the outside world. But that does not mean that the wife of a Muslim man may not be head of state, and a husband may in that respect be under her command.'

JB: 'Why can't the woman represent the family to the outside world?'

'As in the example I gave earlier, Aisha did.'

JB: 'Should that example be the model for Muslim wives now?'

'That example is there and it cannot be argued against. It is not refutable. In that sense it is authority for women, to act in public roles, leading men, and perhaps in preference to less able men. The necessary quality is ability.'

JB: 'What about the meaning of the other verse to which reference is usually made?'

'To translate is to interpret, and there are many interpretations of any Qur'ānic verse and injunction. Profound scholars will offer many different interpretations, and it is then up to the individual Muslim conscience to find the best path, which is the one that is felt, in one's conscience, to be the true path. The verse in question is sura iv. 34: it has many different interpretations, and it is a difficult verse, as many of the verses in the Qur'ān are. Rank, authority, status: a possible interpretation *is* an authoritarian one, but it is not the only one, and even then, with authority goes responsibility, and the Qur'ān reiterates again and again men's responsibility. Authority is a burden rather than a privilege. It is a great sin in fact to exploit authority. We are told that it is the path to damnation.'

In practice then a marriage in which there is not an equality of respect and consultation would be a contradiction of Islam.

Nevertheless, the impression remains to the outsider that Islam gives precedence to the men. There seems to be a lack of symmetry between what is allowed for men and for women. Thus according to the Qur'ān (iv. 3), men are allowed to marry up to four wives, but women are not allowed to marry four husbands; men are allowed to beat their wives (iv. 34/38), the reverse is not true; Muslim men are allowed to marry women who come from the People of the Book, Muslim women are forbidden to marry men from the *ahl al-Kitab*. Islam from the start gave women rights to their own property which, in the case of *mahr*, or the dowry, cannot be appropriated by the husband and is retained if there is a divorce; and in the case of divorce, it allows the woman to take the initiative. But for men, the practice of divorce by way of repudiation, *talaq*, seems much simpler: they have to pronounce 'I divorce you' three times in front of a witness, who is not necessarily the wife, and allow an interval of one month between each pronouncement (to make clear whether a pregnancy is involved; the pronouncement cannot be made during menstruation). The practice of repeating the threefold formula all on one occasion is strongly repudiated by many Muslims, but it has nevertheless become a practice in some areas of Islam.

But what do Muslims really believe about these apparent imbalances between men and women? Or is their appearance as such to the outsider once again the product of a lack of knowledge?

The Beating of Wives

In the case of the husband's right to beat his wife, the point is frequently made that this is a merciful provision, not a severe one:

128

'The verse certainly must be understood literally, and not taken as having some symbolic meaning only. It is literal. And I also say that it is one of the most merciful injunctions in the Qur'ān. To give you the full picture, the injunction is aimed at keeping family life intact. It is an anti-divorce measure. And because it is an anti-divorce measure, it is a merciful measure. It stops families breaking down, it stops children being deprived of one parent or the other. The Qur'ān says that if you fear that a wife is being eccentric – in other words, really out of order, out of balance, being really hysterical, breaking the china, tearing the carpets, pulling down the curtains – then, first of all, you say to her, "Listen, you are not doing the right thing, you are doing the wrong thing." In other words, the Qur'ān says, first advise her. If the advice works, fine. If it does not, then you go a step further. You say, "Listen, you are not behaving like a good wife, therefore I am not going to sleep with you – you go and sleep in the other room." That is to put psychological pressure on her, because she is not behaving rationally and reasonably. If it works, fine. If it does not work, you go a step further, and the step further is that you beat her. You beat her, but not on the face – never touch the face. You beat her with something that does not leave a mark or an injury. The Prophet gave an example: he got two pieces of cloth and put them together, and he said, "Like this".

'In other words, beating her is symbolic. It does not mean that you hang her by her hair from the chandelier and beat her with a big cane or anything like that. You beat her, yes, but as a kind of physical pressure, if the psychological pressure does not work, to bring her to her senses. You do not abuse her with words, you do not say, "You are ugly, you are a cow" – this is forbidden. For God's sake, what is more harmful than to say that she is a cow, that she is ugly, she is fat? Now all this is merciful because divorce is easy in Islam. The door is wide open for a woman or a man who wants to come out of marriage. So the husband who goes through all these steps is showing that he loves his wife. If he did not, the door is open for divorcing her. It is anti-divorce and therefore it is merciful.'

JB: 'Then why can't the woman take the same merciful action towards the husband?'

'Partly she can. We come to another part of the Qur'ān which says that if a wife fears that her husband is going to be eccentric, there is the same measure for the wife too. She can advise him first – they always do. Psychological pressure of withdrawing closeness and intimacy? Well, the wife more often than not does that when she wants to. But physical pressure, like a very symbolic smack or something? Well, the wife is physically inferior, generally speaking; she is not as strong as the man. So the wife is not required to beat her husband. But she has use of an injunction which is better than that, which is to sit down with the rest of the community, if need be with a judge, and draw up a contract with the man, which says: You have done this or that – if you do it again, this will be the consequence. In other words, she is getting the community behind her.'

So the verse is literally intended, but the action is symbolic, and it always has an extrinsic purpose:

'The verse in the Qur'ān had to do with a specific situation where the husband was afraid that the wife was being unfaithful. This used to happen in those days when the discrepancy in ages was very great. In the pre-Islamic days, a man would then beat his wife severely. The Prophet, in contrast, said that no man should ever touch or harm his wife; and he never touched any one of his wives at all. So the Qur'ān specifies that a man may not harm his wife, he may not touch her face; in fact some of the scholars said that he would have to use a handkerchief. So really

I think that people exaggerate. They read the one verse without appreciating the enormous explanations that go with it.'

So what *is* the meaning of that verse in its more general context?

'A husband and a wife are responsible for each other's spiritual growth and development. They are responsible for each other's salvation. One of the interpretations of that verse, which is a difficult one, is that a husband who is executing legal judgement in that way upon his wife is thus sparing her public humiliation. One of the penalties for adultery in the Qur'ān is a public flogging, a public beating. The beating is an exercise in public humiliation, and is not intended to cause pain or injury, because the person who is doing the flogging must hold a copy of the Qur'ān under his elbow. So one interpretation of that verse is that it is the husband who chastizes his wife for infidelity in that way, in private.'

JB: 'Then why can't a woman do the same to the man? It is clearly not a matter of physical strength, if the action is symbolic, as it is.'

'As I understand it, there are interpretations which argue that, but men as a rule do have a public role, and men have a greater freedom of movement, particularly where women have children. They have therefore greater responsibility.'

Polygamy

But should this difference in roles and responsibility extend to polygamy for men but not the equivalent for women? Islam, like many cultures, places great emphasis on paternity and lineage in establishing the structure of society. It is a matter of knowing who and what belongs to whom. It is this which underlies the permission (not the obligation) for men to have more than one wife:

The reason is quite simple: you want to know the father of the child. The mother is unmistakably established in the whole act of procreation. The mother is known. It is the father who would otherwise be uncertain, if a woman married more than one husband.

JB: 'But supposing it were now possible to establish easily, and in ways that were readily available, the genetic paternity of any child, would that open up the possibility that a woman might marry more than one husband?'

'Oh no, I am afraid that that is going beyond our limits; no, no. There are really social reasons against it, which apply in every society. Polygamy is permitted and not made an obligation – though some societies have limited it; in Tunisia, for example, it is not allowed at all, and that is supported by the ulama in that country. In Pakistan, a man may not marry another wife without the permission of the first wife, and that permission has to be given in writing. In this country [Britain], we have a certificate of marriage in which the wife can stipulate that she will not allow the husband to take another wife. So the possibility of polygamy can be dealt with on the basis of Islamic law. It has a foundation in Muslim law which people do not realize: when the Prophet married his daughter to his cousin 'Alī, and 'Alī after a few years decided that he would like to have another wife, the Prophet went into the pulpit and said, "I am not going to allow my daughter to have another woman sharing her husband." Many people think that the same should apply to their daughters as well.'

Still, polygamy remains a possibility because the Qur'ān sanctions it. On the other hand, it sanctions it in a way that may in effect make it impossible. It requires that each wife must be treated equally:

The permission goes along with an injunction to treat each

wife equally, which is interpreted by many scholars – though not all scholars – to suggest that, being human, a man cannot possibly have more than one wife, because it is not humanly possible to treat them equally. My own feeling is that since marriage in Islam is a spiritual relationship, husband and wife being responsible for each other's spiritual development, and that as men and women are as a garment to one another and comfort one another, it would be very difficult for me to imagine that kind of relationship with more than one adult.'

Divorce

What then of the apparent lack of symmetry where divorce is concerned?

'There are different types of divorce, one in which the man instigates the divorce, one in which the woman instigates the divorce, and another in which the court instigates the divorce. The one that everybody knows about is the one that the man instigates. But that is only one of many forms. If the husband feels that he cannot live with his wife any longer, then firstly, the Qur'ān says, he has to appoint two arbitrators, one from each side of the family, to sit down and discuss their problems. That is often forgotten – nobody does that, although it is very important. But if that fails, the husband is allowed to say, in a written form or a spoken form, "I wish to divorce you". He has to say that when the woman is in a state of purity, when she is not menstruating. A month later, if he wishes to carry on, he can say the second divorce, and again he has another month to think about it, and if he then pronounces the third divorce, they are divorced. They cannot live together after that. The Prophet said that the triple divorce statements have to be spread over three months, to give them a chance to think again. What happened later was that because of a particular incident, people accepted the three divorce statements being made at one moment. That is clearly wrong. The problem is that the majority of Muslims follow that, but it is wrong, it is as simple as that.'

JB: 'If a woman instigates the divorce, is the procedure the same?'

'No, it is different. It is actually much easier for a woman to get a divorce, because she just needs to go to a judge, to a *qadi*, and say that for these reasons she would like a divorce, and he can give the divorce – though he too must try to get them to discuss their problems.'

JB: 'How often does it happen that way round – say, in the UK?'

'There is an Islamic Sharia Council in this country, which does not have legislative powers, but exists to help Muslims. Something like ninety-five per cent of its work is with women coming and saying, "I want a divorce." Women do take the initiative, but the problem is that many women do not know that they have this right – the number of women I have had to say this to, "You've got that right!" Many Muslim women do not know that they have the right to get a divorce.'

JB: 'How in practice can you change that?'

'In practice, all we can do is educate, that's all we can do.'

The Rights of Women

And here we are once more back to the same general point: if there are rights of women according to Sharia, and if women are being treated differently and wrongly, then Muslims in saying this are setting an agenda for themselves. In talking to the outsider in order to educate him or her, they are also talking to themselves in order to educate each other, and in order to recover Islam from its misinterpretation:

'Since men have had the greater social power and authority, they are naturally going to interpret laws in one particular way, to suit themselves, and I don't think this is a particular Muslim problem; it is a universal problem.'

JB: 'But you use the word problem.'

'Yes, I think it is a problem when, as a result of this, women are denied their rights – rights to education, to the free exercise of their talents and their faculties, and to the use of their money, their property and their wealth, and to the care of their children – as might happen when a wife is divorced, sometimes without her knowledge. These are abuses of Muslim law.'

JB: 'Where there are abuses, what avenues of action are open to those who wish to put an end to them, both for those who are in the situation, and for other Muslims, who observe them from the outside?'

'I think one of the most important weapons, shall we say, for Muslim women, is knowledge and understanding of Muslim law, and this is dependent on education. So in a sense one could say that it is circular: if a woman is denied education, she won't be aware of her rights, and not being aware of her rights she will be more vulnerable and less likely to be educated. The most obvious and straightforward defence for women in these situations is an application of the law.'

The way forward is the way back – to Sharia, where women's rights are specified and protected. But there is no doubt that the process of recovering Sharia (which is *not* a matter of returning to the past but of creating a future which Sharia enables) will be painful, and it will be resisted by those who prefer cultural clothes to Muslim obedience, as one Muslim has already observed. When I went on to ask him which aspects of Muslim life as it is now lived will have to change, he replied:

'Those that are to do with the social system. Most of the Sharia laws were written under the Abbasids and towards the end of the Umayyads. So they reflect the society of the time. These aspects have to go – for example, the treatment of women. The position of women in society will most certainly change. Now the Muslim scholars had many arguments about the position of women in society, which is not generally known – in Muslim circles as much as outside Muslim circles. One of the most famous of our scholars is at-Tabari, who was a historian and a commentator on the Qur'ān, and who was also a collector of Traditions. In that respect, he was better qualified than any of the founders of the schools. His attitude towards women was that a woman is not to be barred from any office of the state. But because his ideas did not reflect the social situation as it then existed, his school never prospered. What is going to happen in the future? We will certainly change our attitude to women, most certainly. Our ideas of social organization and human relations will certainly also change.'

But all that requires an immense effort in self and community education. Can it happen? Does it require separate Muslim schools if it is to happen? What *do* Muslims believe about education?

CHAPTER FIVE

EDUCATION AND FREEDOM OF ENQUIRY

The way forward for Muslims is the way back, so Muslims have been telling us repeatedly: back to Sharia. That is by no means as obscurantist as it may seem – as a phrase. Sharia is the application of the Qur'ān and Hadith in a way that does not fix or freeze Muslim life in sixth-century Arabia, but opens it to new interpretation and to application to new circumstances or discoveries. The Muslims we have been listening to have been saying that if only *all* Muslims would understand what Sharia really says, and how it is open to creative application, then Islam would be seen for what it should be, the perfect model of well-ordered life and society:

'The people of belief have especial responsibilities. I am sure that if we work together, and are seen to be working together, then we can create a society in Britain which would be exemplary to the rest of the world.'

The Aims and Absolutes of Education

But this requires a massive programme of self and community education among Muslims. Muslim education is not just education *about* Islam. The aims of education in Islam are much deeper than that:

'To start with, in Islam, education is the chance to acquire knowledge and a refinement of character, because knowledge in Islam has practical connotations. If somebody knows a lot of information and does not live by it, he is likened to a donkey carrying books. We believe that every human should have the right to the best possible education. Every human being should have the right to develop to the best of his or her capacity. It is also very important to state that, in a child's education, the parents should have the ultimate say, while the child is still a minor. The child has been born to those parents and it is not common property, of a kind that the government can educate and re-educate as it likes. Parents' wishes, particularly with regard to ideology or religion, have to be taken into account and have to be honoured. This would even apply to an Islamic state, where, if parents wanted to bring up their children in any other religion, the state would have to permit that.'

This emphasis on the responsibilities of parents (and thus on rights derived from those responsibilities) goes back to the Qur'ān and to its statement that all children are a consequence of the will and purpose of God: 'To God belongs sovereignty over the heavens and the earth. He creates what He wills. He bestows to whom He wills males, and He bestows to whom He wills females, or He unites them, males and females, and He makes whom He wills barren. Surely He is all-knowing, all-powerful' (xlii. 48–9). It follows also, from the fact that there is no concept of radical sin or fault in Islam, that education is vital in the forming of life and behaviour which will be rewarded by God on the Day of Judgement. In the formation of character, it is inevitable that Islam will give high and deliberate priority to moral education, in a way that is remote from – to take an obvious example – the introduction of the National Curriculum in the UK:

'There are only two absolutes: one is your spirit, and the other is the reality of the absolute values, and they are tied up with your spirit. I'll explain it in this way: little children, whom you have not taught anything – you have not taught them theories of right and wrong – what is the response of those children if you slap them unjustly? They know that something wrong has been done to them. That means that in them, in their own being, they have a sense of right and wrong. Why do they respond to love? What is the response to goodness and badness when you talk to little children – and the response to the way you talk, when you ask them to give something to a destitute person, for example? What sort of feeling emerges? Are not these sort of things inherent in every human being, inherent in the human spirit? So the absolute values are inherent. We have a metaphysical explanation of that, and that explanation is exactly similar to the explanation that you have in Christianity, in Hinduism and in every religion – it is in the religious tradition of the world. Therefore, when we say "absolutes" in relation to education, we mean two things: one is the spiritual condition or nature which we all have, and the other is the development and the rearing of the spiritual sensibility, which ultimately gives certainty to human beings. So in brief, I can say that Islamic education is education that trains the total personality so that men and women can become true servants of God.'

Education and the Qur'ān

However, since the Qur'ān is the direct expression of the will of God for the behaviour of His creatures, it follows that Islamic education will necessarily be grounded in the Qur'ān:

'A profound knowledge of the Qur'ān is *the* most important thing in education. All these university degrees are worth nothing if a Muslim does not know what the Qur'ān says. The goal of education, from a very young age, should be to teach children, not just to recite the Qur'ān in Arabic, but to know what every single word says, and to know what the Hadith are – from a very, very young age, they have got to know the Qur'ān and the Sunna.'

The reference to the recitation of the Qur'ān without understanding it summons up the picture, often exhibited in the media, of rows of children learning to chant by rote something that is meaningless to them. There is a virtue in Islam in reciting the Qur'ān for its own sake, in the traditional way. If the Qur'ān is a kind of music (see chapter 2), there can be a value in the performance of it, quite apart from issues of understanding.

Nevertheless, the Muslim view is that learning the Qur'ān by rote, without any aim at all of understanding it at some point, is clearly wrong:

'In the methodology of education, we often find that the way that Islam is taught to people is through rote learning. It is through the memorization of the Qur'ān, and things like that. I become very angry when I see programmes on television where they visit a school, say in Bradford, and the teachers are seen teaching them the Qur'ān, and you have a lot of children swaying back and forth, saying something that they don't understand. The net result is that we have our imams and our ulama graduating, leading the *juma* [weekly] Friday prayer, and reciting from a fixed book which was actually written in the Abbasid times, praising the Abbasid Caliph, and they read it in Arabic, and they do not understand what they are saying in Arabic. Often I go to these mosques and I listen, and because I know some Arabic, I understand it, and I feel like laughing, and I don't gain the benefit of what the Friday prayer is meant to be: an exhortation, to remind you of your religion and to send you away recharged for the rest of the week. So the net effect of the Islamic style of education – and I am just using the words: this is *not* Islamic education as it is meant to be – the net effect is less than it should be. But the mistakes of this kind of Islamic education must realized, and it must be realized that understanding is much better. There is a saying of the Prophet that one hour spent in contemplating the creation of the universe is better than a thousand years spent in prayer. That emphasizes that the understanding of what we learn is far more important than the memorization.'

Nevertheless, the First World Conference on Muslim Education, which was held in Mecca in 1977, was entirely clear as to what the aim of Muslim education is:

> The ultimate aim of Muslim education lies in the realization of complete submission to Allah on the level of the individual, the community and humanity at large.

It follows that the content of education must be controlled by Sharia – or so the Conference went on to state:

> In order to achieve the ultimate aims and objectives of education, knowledge [is to] be classified into the following two categories: (a) Revealed 'perennial knowledge' based on the divine revelation presented in the Qur'ān and Sunna and all that can be derived from them, with emphasis on the Arabic language as the key to the understanding of both. (b) 'Acquired knowledge', including social, natural and applied science susceptible to quantitative growth and multiplication, and limited variations and cross-cultural borrowings as long as consistency with the Sharia as the source of values is maintained. There must be a core knowledge drawn from both with major emphasis on the first, especially on the Sharia, which must be made obligatory to all Muslims at all levels of the educational system from the highest to the

lowest . . . This, along with the compulsory teaching of Arabic, should form the major section of the core curriculum. These two alone can sustain Islamic civilization and preserve the identity of the Muslims.

The Scope of Islamic Education

Given the foundations in the Qur'ān and Hadith, from which the control of Sharia is derived, it is then clear that Islamic education cannot – and should not – be confined to theological education and to *fiqh* (Islamic jurisprudence), as it was for many centuries. From the outset, Islam was committed to *'ilm*, or knowledge. *'Ilm* is a fundamental value in the Qur'ān, as indeed it must be, since the universe is God's creation. To understand it, therefore, is to understand the signs of God's creative act; the very word *ayat* refers to both the verses of the Qur'ān and the evidence of God in creation – both are revelations, in their own way. So if the universe and the wisdom to understand it come from God, it cannot be an offence to be committed to openness and integrity of enquiry. It was spectacularly so in the early centuries, as I have pointed out at length in *The Religious Imagination and the Sense of God* (Oxford University Press, 1978):

> Traces of the Arab renaissance have left their mark in the English language, not least in the fact that we refer to 'arabic numerals', but also in words which begin with the arabic article 'al' (the Arabic word for 'the'), such as algebra, alkali, almanac, alHambra, alembic, algorithm, alchemy, and in many names of the stars. (p. 198)

Muslim philosophers rescued the Greek tradition for the West, and extended it greatly. It was only later, after the time of al-

Ghazali, that philosophy and science receded, and that *fiqh* and theology became exclusively dominant:

'It is fair to say that the philosophical tradition of Islam is dead at the moment. We do not have a philosophical tradition now. We have not had one for the last five centuries. But I think it is there. There are passages in the medieval and early Arab philosophers, people like al-Ghazali, al-Kindi, ibn Rushd [Averroes], which are philosophical in the modern sense of the word, not just in the Eastern sense of "full of wisdom". They are susceptible to that interpretation.'

The importance of recovering that Islamic integration of understanding and character is that it would, in the Muslim view, contribute to prevailing philosophies of education a dimension which is at present disastrously missing: it would include within the educational domain, as a matter of its concern, the religious character of human beings and of the universe:

'Until very recently, whenever we used to talk of Islamic education, we used to mean mainly theological education – just the teaching of the Qur'ān and the Sunna and the Hadith and the *tafsir* [commentary on Qur'ān], all theological things. After the First World Conference on Islamic Education, it has become more common to talk of education which is to be Islamic in character. That is going back to the essence, which is completely denied, in a way, in all Western educational systems, and which has become dominant also in the East, in Pakistan or Bangladesh or wherever. Wherever the British went, they spread this new education system, which they wanted to be neutral. Neutral meant that they wanted it to be secular. So all the origins of modern knowledge eliminate one source, and that is the spiritual source. So it is a limited form of education which is given to us, and that other aspect of human nature does not develop. On the other hand, we become very logical and reasoning, but we want only demonstrable proofs – of a kind that can be materially given to us. But the spiritual is another domain which is also necessary, and there should be an integrated approach to education. That is what we want. And for that, conceptual work is already going on. We have already prepared syllabuses, from the age of five to sixteen. We are using, for example, the National Curriculum science syllabus, and we are altering and modifying it to express this integrated character.'

So the aim of Islamic education is to produce a well-ordered society with morally responsible and well-informed citizens; and also to be an exploration of history and the universe through appropriate disciplines. But a secularized history and science tell only a distorted part of the story:

'Let me tell you this, every particular aspect of something has to be understood according to the nature of that thing. Isn't that so? So if, for example, you want to analyse words in poetry, and then throw the words in a crucible like a chemist, you won't get the meaning of it. If you only look up words in a dictionary in order to appreciate poetry, you won't grasp its meaning. There is an emotive element in poetry: poetry wants to move us, to give us some understanding of the truth which the writer has felt. The use of scientific method destroys poetry. Thus the structuralist critics tried to criticize poetry from the point of view of the structure of words and phrases. Some of that criticism was quite good, but they went too far in not recognizing anything further, and they destroyed the poetry altogether. So one cannot apply the same method for everything.'

Values in Education

Since no education is value-free, the most important thing, in the Muslim perception, is to choose the right values to be embodied in the educational system in the first place:

'I think that clearly in a school you are going to put over a certain message. You are educating people, you are teaching them something. You must have a certain moral philosophy. There is definitely a philosophy of education current in general in comprehensive schools in England; there is a slightly different philosophy in the public schools. As Muslims we have a philosophy of education, a certain viewpoint which we would like the children to see. It is not that we are going to be dogmatic and only present that viewpoint, but it would be silly to say that science or knowledge is purely objective and value-free, and that there are no subjective views going into it. So as Muslims, we want to recognize that fact and present all sciences and subjects from a Muslim viewpoint.'

The recognition that the natural sciences are not themselves value-free is a very recent event. There are many non-Muslims who accept some version of scientism without realizing how deeply flawed it is. The Muslim argument is that children need to be trained to recognise embodied values from the outset:

'It is important not to exaggerate the degrees of freedom in education. I do not think, for example, enquiry is free at most universities in the Western world. There is a clear direction of research – it depends on who is paying the grants for it, and so on. If you could make any education fully value-neutral, then it might be a valid accusation against the Muslims that they want their values to underlie education. I think it is an illegitimate demand on Muslims that they should be fairer than most people are in their teaching. Isn't it true of teaching in general? When I was trained as a philosopher, I remember that all the lecturers had their own biases. If they thought that a particular view was one that they did not want us to adopt, they always taught it with prejudicial rigour. What would be wrong would be for any school to refuse to teach anything that they thought was subversive. After something has been taught, even if it has been taught badly, it is up to the children to decide in later life whether it is true or not.'

JB: 'But is it true that a Muslim daughter, when she comes of age, is absolutely free in that way?'

'No, I don't think she is absolutely free, but I don't know of any other daughters who are. This is really a question of comparing the degree and the extent to which different models of education inculcate freedom of conviction or freedom of conscience, and so on.'

If the same values are embodied in all religions, it follows that there could be no Muslim objection to learning about all, or at least some, other religions:

'I don't think the best way is to mix the children of different religions, but to prepare them mentally for the society at large in which they live. That can be done in many different ways, but one is to introduce a curriculum which is just and fair, and which creates and promotes understanding and harmony. We are not objecting to teaching our children about other faiths. We want Muslim children to learn about Christianity and about other faiths. We do not want them to convert to any other religion, and we have no intention to convert the other people to ours. To learn even briefly what Hinduism means – there's nothing wrong in that. And this is something which we are lacking at the moment, which ought to be introduced. They will be better citizens with each other after that.'

Muslim Schools?

That last statement began with the belief that it is wrong to mix up children of different religions in the same school. That is a way of expressing the widespread demand of Muslims in Britain that they should have their own state-supported schools, as Christians and Jews already do – indeed, Christians of different denominations have their own schools. Why not the Muslims, even if only as a matter of equity under the existing law?

'When someone talks about separate Muslim schools, I get alarmed, because nobody talks about separate Church of England or Roman Catholic schools. They talk about denominational schools. Why can't we talk about Muslim denominational schools, rather than separate schools? According to the 1944 Education Act, reinforced by the 1988 Act, religious groups have a right to establish their own denominational schools; and as long as they are allowed by law, there should be equal treatment. At the moment, the way in which the law is applied means that the Muslims have not been treated fairly and justly.'

JB: 'One reason why people are inclined to use the word "separate" is because they look at Northern Ireland and see denominational schools reinforcing the separation and hostility of two religious communities, or at least, not making a noticeable contribution to a peaceful society. Why would we want to extend that further?'

'I visited Northern Ireland years ago, in order to find out for myself. I was open and clear, and I asked various searching and difficult questions of each group. And after two days there, to be quite honest, if you had been in my position you would have come out as confused as you went in. Both sides could justify their case, and each side was blaming the other. But one thing was pretty clear: it was not the fault of their separate schools. It is the deep-rooted prejudice there, which is very complicated indeed, but is not to do with the schools.'

The more important Muslim claim is that their own schools

in the state system would be a major contribution to contesting the evils and injustices of society, because of the spiritual and moral values which would be embodied in both the curriculum and the community:

'I would argue that if boys and girls were taught separately in Muslim schools, according to the proper manner in the Qur'ān, that would be the best thing that the immigrant community could give to Britain. I will tell you why: if Muslim children are educated and instructed properly in their own language, you will have students, girls or boys, who are gentle, who are just, who treat their neighbours well, who are good as workers, who work hard, who are not vandals or drunkards, they won't drink and drive, kill, or rape. We would benefit a lot by having the children taught the proper Islamic religion. Britain as a society would gain a great deal from having the Muslims follow their religion properly, not the other way round. There has been a myth that the Islamic religion is a bad religion, and that the quicker we get the second generation Muslim children out of the religion, the better for Britain. What a very dangerous myth! It's the other way round. The sooner we get Muslim children to live their religion, the safer Britain will be. We don't need any more drug addicts or vandals or hooligans, we've got enough already.'

JB: 'Are you saying that in countries where there are Muslim schools, there are none of these anti-social behaviours?'

'I think you will probably find that if you ask the tourists who come from Muslim countries, they will tell you that they feel far safer there than anywhere else in the world.'

The Separation of Boys and Girls

The first sentence of that argument introduced another point of well-known importance, the Muslim view that it is better, and indeed necessary, to separate boys and girls during education. That is partly because there are differences in nature, which lead to different aptitudes and interests (the argument that these might be acquired culturally is foreclosed by that other argument about nature):

'I think you will find that girls do better in "girls-only" schools. And boys do better in "boys-only" schools. I have been told by teachers, who have worked in both, that when there is a mixed school, what boys do all the time is hang around girls. But when they are in "boys-only" schools they play more sport, they behave more like boys and they are less inhibited. Girls are also severely inhibited in mixed schools. They do not do as well. They look on the boys in their class as their superiors. They don't do sciences, they don't go for the same subjects as the boys, and even if they do, they don't have a go in the same way that the boys do, say, in the computer room. So, from the practical point of view, I think it is a myth that it is better for society that boys and girls should come together at an early age.'

But quite apart from that kind of consideration, the separation is necessary because of the basic principle underlying so much of the Sharia, of preventing sin even coming up to the threshold through possibility or temptation:

'The campaign for separate schools is not a part of any distinctively religious imperative. It is a question of equality under the law. What are the reasons for wanting separate schooling? I think there is a fear, particularly in the case with daughters, that Western society has become unduly permissive in its ethics, and that Christianity has lost control of some of the subversive elements. It is no longer controlling some of these developments. And therefore, if Muslims are to avoid contamination or attenuation of their faithful heritage, they must somehow be able to bring up their children in the right atmosphere.'

But how can that be reconciled with the Muslim argument that separated education is to prepare children for living together in the modern world? How will Muslims, Jews, Hindus and so on, learn to live together if they are all in separate schools?

'They will learn on the buses and in the playground and sitting together in cafés and restaurants, and talking to each other over the garden fence. It is not an enclave at all.'

JB: 'Are you saying that Muslim girls are really free to go to the cafés to mix with their friends?'

'Muslim girls do go to any place they want to. Of course, they don't go on their own in the same loose way that some people do. We want them to be liberal, but we don't want them to be loose. The need for Muslim schools has arisen because of the state of education in the state schools, and also because of the new injunctions on religious education. The new law actually emphasizes the differences between religions, rather than the common ground. What I want from religious education is that it should teach children the shared ethical ground which is held in common between the three [Western] religions – common between all religions – and that is the moral way of life. I want the religious education teacher to produce a proper little individual, to help us and not to be a threat to us. I don't want the religious education teacher to concentrate on Muslims wearing a cap like this and Jews wearing a cap like that. This is trivialization of religion. I want the general ethical and moral ground of religion to be taught.'

Secular World-View and Islam

And there perhaps is the crux: Muslims cannot trust their children to secular ideologies, which eliminate God and turn out (at least so far) to be unstable and short-lived enthusiasms. The failure of Communism as an ideology does not take Muslims by surprise, nor does the necessity to contest it. But does that contest extend to other aspects of a secular world-view? What is the resolution in education to be if the natural sciences seem to conflict, in detail or in ethos, with the Qur'ān? The Qur'ān speaks of Adam and Eve, for example, as real people, the parents of the human race, and of Adam as the first prophet. But post-Darwinian theories of evolution (which are not thought by anyone to be complete or incorrigible, but which have considerable evidential support, to say the very least) envisage a much longer process of human emergence. Is there a conflict?

The general Muslim answer is to say that there cannot be any conflicts between the Qur'ān and science, because both come from God:

'Scientific discoveries have brought us nearer and nearer to the truth which the Qur'ān contains. It has very detailed statements, unlike any other religious book, which are not at all in contradiction with the real state of affairs in the natural world around us. Unfortunately, in the Christian sphere, science and religion have been at odds throughout, because the Church, following a very narrow interpretation of the religious law, opposed scientific experiments and scientific investigation and research. Naturally, scientists and researchers opposed the Church, and it seemed as though science and religion could not go together, which is very, very unfortunate. In Islam, religion and science complement each other. Actually, the Qur'ān was the original motivating force for Muslims to do scientific investigations. The whole Age of Enlightenment started from the Muslim countries, and was brought to us from Spain. The Qur'ān is full of scientific explanations, which only now, in modern science, are understood in their full depth; and it is realized that these statements cannot in any way have been made without divine knowledge, because they are so accurate. Nobody, fourteen hundred years ago, could have made them and invented them in their mind.'

Adam and Eve and Evolution

There are obviously some contestable claims in that statement. But in general, it makes the point about necessary coherence. So what about the *apparent* conflict between evolution and the reality of Adam and Eve? One response is to say that evolution is clearly wrong, and to stress that there are many gaps in the fossil evidence:

'The Qur'ān says that Adam and Eve were real people, created from the dust, a man and a woman, and they were sent down as our first parents, so yes, they were a real man and a woman.'

JB: 'How does that relate to theories of a gradual evolution?'

'Having studied evolution years and years ago, at school, I can say that the gaps in the chain – the so-called missing link – are so great that I am sorry but I don't accept it. Scientifically it is completely false.'

JB: 'Supposing the missing link turned up?'

'I don't think it will: that's my private opinion. It can't, because the Qur'ān says very clearly why the world was created. It was created to serve men and women, so that human beings can profit from all the gifts and bounties which God has given to us in this world, in order to serve Him. So evolution does not really come into it.'

The 'missing link' argument against evolution is then reinforced by a claim that consciousness and the mind require a special creation – the possibility that they might be emergent properties of a complex organization does not appeal:

'The Darwinian theory has not been proved. It is only a theory in which the evidence has so many gaps, and those gaps have never been filled. There are several eminent modern scientists who have criticized the theory of evolution, but the theory has become a dogma everywhere. However, how do you prove the theory of evolution? I will ask a simple question: science says, logically, that if a particular element is not there in a particular object, it cannot create that element in it. That is logical, is it not? If that is so, then where did consciousness and intelligence come from if this whole human being developed from an unconscious cell? Darwin, in his *Origin of Species*, said, "This eyesight: I cannot explain how this eyesight came about." It is not merely eyesight, but also human intelligence, which itself does all this theorizing; where did this come from? So logically, it is an absurd theory. But if you think of Adam having his body built and then God infusing it – if we put it in metaphysical terms – then you have an infusion of matter by a super-intelligence. So that is how the body got its intelligence. Otherwise the intelligence cannot develop: matter cannot create that intelligence.'

In this style of response, there cannot possibly be a conflict; and if it looked as though there might be, that in itself would be a reason for abandoning that line of enquiry or research:

'Personally, having accepted Islam wholeheartedly, I cannot see a conflict happening. That's my feeling, that God has created us, and He knows us better than anyone will ever know us, and what He says is what we need to hear. If there is a conflict, I don't know what we would have to do – maybe abandon that research.'

Yet in fact Islam, with its strong sense of creation, is

exceptionally well placed to see the universe as an unfolding revelation of God, which extends or at least provides an informative commentary on the Qur'ān. And there are Muslims who take exactly that position:

'We believe that Adam and Eve were real people. That is the common belief. We accept the literal interpretation. They spoke to God in the same way that I speak to you.'

JB: 'How does that cohere with evolutionary, developmental ideas of the emergence of humans?'

'In the last century, a scholar from Aleppo wrote treatises on this which are rather endearing. He said, "Look, we are hearing about Darwinism, which is creating such a storm in the West, but these developments – the idea that we were produced through stages – do not necessarily militate against the Qur'ān. It is still a theory," he said. "It is not an absolute fact. But if it should prove, later on, to be a fact and be supported conclusively by scientific evidence, we need not be worried about the text of the Qur'ān, because the Qur'ān itself says that God has created man from earth. That is really describing whole stages of development, and when man came, that first man or first creation may have participated in that particular drama." That is one interpretation. The other possible interpretation, which is a much older one and was not referring to Darwinism at all, treated most of these stories as symbolic. They are not really persons or individual situations, but rather they represent the relationship between man and God, and therefore Adam becomes the human race, rather than just an individual person. The whole drama is to describe the relation between man and God.'

So far as schools and education are concerned, there would be teaching about evolution, but always under the control of the Qur'ān:

'If we Muslims were in a majority, I have to admit that, yes, we would lay down certain limits to what we would allow to be taught in schools; and certainly, if we taught something such as atheism or even Hinduism, we would teach it in the sense of saying that it exists, while pointing out what we see as the faults in it, just as we would point out in the case of Darwinian evolution the validity of a lot of what he said, while also pointing out that it is a theory that is not proven, so that as Muslims, we do not accept very basic parts of it.'

JB: 'How do you decide what is valid and what is not, in a theory of evolution?'

'Well, there's got to be two ways of looking at things, I think. First and foremost, the revelation, the revealed books right the way through from the Bible to the Qur'ān which we see as the final statement, together with the sayings of the Prophet, are the primary source of what is right and wrong, and about the creation. However, that does not say very much about detailed matters, such as genetic engineering and nuclear physics. So the second way is through trial and error, by scientific experimentation, by theory-creation, and by attempts to prove those theories. This was pioneered in Muslim Spain where there was a certain amount of research going on into medical sciences; and the scientific method, we could argue, came from there to the West. So the scientific method we certainly do not reject. But what I am saying is that theories must be seen as theories. Darwinian theory is not a Darwinian fact. So we are not obliged to accept any part of it. However, it is the best-fitting theory that we have.'

JB: 'But if it conflicted with the Qur'ān, would it, *ipso facto*, be false?'

'Certainly those parts that conflicted with the Qur'ān would be false if they involved something basic and fundamental, and

155

not just an interpretation (we must be clear that what we are saying is "from the Qur'ān") – but if there were something in the Qur'ān which contradicted what Darwin has said, then we would not accept the theory, but we would accept the fact, and that is the Qur'ān.'

Yet even so, the voice of individual interpretation speaks up. Islam is not a Vatican-type religion. It is not even a credal religion in the sense that Christianity is. Muslims may pray and worship together in a uniform manner, but they do not recite a creed together on every liturgical occasion; and the individual appropriation (or refusal) is respected provided it does not enact a subversion of Islam, or a threat to the state. I asked three different people the same question, whether the Qur'ān requires them to believe that Adam and Eve were real people:

'Ha! I don't know. And in some sense, I have to say, maybe through some peculiar quirk in my own psychology, I don't find it important.'

'My personal understanding is that it is a story with a spiritual meaning. I personally don't see it as a literal story. But I would tell it to my children in the sense in which a child would understand it. There are many different levels of interpretation of the Qur'ān which are appropriate to different levels of spiritual search.'

'I personally feel that the really crucial question here is to do with whether we believe in the monogenetic origins of the human race. Whether it is through Adam and Eve or through some other way is not of any great consequence. What is important, however, is not to embrace any morality which says that the human race is of more than one origin, which would be to say that differences of race or colour affect and alter human nature in some way. That would be my concern. I don't think it matters particularly what you say. I think the creation story is a matter of convention, really, more than anything else, and it is an easy way of grasping the issue, for most people. I think in that sense Scripture can be interpreted at several different levels. Personally, I would have no great problem in believing that Adam and Eve were real people, because I think that religion asks us to believe in enough incredible things for us to have had some practice in believing this too.'

This brings us back, yet again, to exactly the same point. Islam is concerned with relatively simple and practical beliefs, which are worked into patterns of ordered life. It is not standing around with boxes of matches, waiting to set fire to non-conformists. That makes the Rushdie protest – or rather the non-Muslim reaction to it – all the more tragic, because it is a failure to understand what is offensive, what has gone beyond the bounds of the compromises between cultures, which are taken for granted and legislated for in other domains. The reaction, by refusing to allow the validity of belief, of enlightened twentieth-century people forming their identity and values religiously, has transformed the issue into one of freedom of speech. To Muslims, that is not the issue. The issue is one of the boundaries of offence, and of what kind of remedies are appropriate when the boundary has been transgressed. As Muslims have already insisted (see chapter 3), all freedoms are relative and limited, and must be so.

The Self-Education of Muslims and the Recovery of Islam

The issue within Islam, however, is clear and unavoidable: the Qur'ān sets its own limit on absolute freedom. It always acts as a constraint on authentic Islamic utterance, no matter what kind of interpretation is endorsed, but it does not dictate Islamic utterance. There *are* different kinds of interpretation, and different consequences of interpretation even within the same style. One result of this is that Islam is always likely to be a coalition of extremely diverse expressions of itself. Thus, although I have been asking questions as an outsider and non-Muslim in order to find out what Muslims really believe about authority and jihad and evolution and marriage and education and all the rest of it, the Muslims who answered those questions have been unanimous and consistent on one point: *Muslims also need to know the answers to them.* They have not been uncritical about many aspects of Islam, but in response, they have been saying that the way forward for Islam is the way back to the recovery of what God intended, which is mapped in the schools of Sharia. Whatever word might be appropriate to describe this proposal, the word 'fundamentalism' is absolutely and unequivocally not the right one. Sharia carries with it the necessity and the procedures for exegesis and development. Sharia, to be appropriated into life, has to be applied to a world of constantly new discoveries, all of which are an exploration of God's own work of creation, none of which therefore (if true) can be threatening, and some of which will require very considerable changes in Muslim practice. If that is to happen (and Islam cannot be itself if it does not), then Muslims are clearly setting for themselves a massive agenda, not just of understanding what Sharia would mean today, but in extending that understanding in practice into the Muslim world at large.

Would that involve the correction of those abuses or contradictions of Islam which exist, and which all the Muslims I spoke with recognize as existing? They were clear that that is indeed a part of the agenda. What is not at all clear is how Muslims move towards this correction, given the necessary toleration of diversity within the ethos of Islam. Where and how will the same kind of concerted action appear, which appeared in relation to *The Satanic Verses* – but this time, action against the contradictions of Islam by Muslims themselves? Or, more positively, where and how will concerted action appear among Muslims on behalf of the beleaguered planet? Islam is a vision of umma, of human community to which is entrusted the trusteeship or stewardship of the planet. What an ideology for the good of us all if it were put into living and practical effect! As one Muslim put it, when I asked him what his dream is for Islam in the new century:

'My dream for Islam is that the Muslim world should not get stuck in some kind of static, antagonistic attitude to the non-Muslim world, but will realize that one can learn and engage, that culture is a living organism which is always changing; it is not something where you say, "Here we are, we've crystallized it, this is it, we're not going to move." It doesn't happen that way. It's going to be changing. My dream – second point – is for Islam to engage seriously with its own history, and not reject certain aspects by saying, "Oh, that's unIslamic!" It's been fashionable, for example, to reject the great philosophers of Islam on the grounds that they were not really Muslims, they were talking about Plato and so on. No, they were very important and they will enrich our lives. I would also like to see the fundamental idea of Islam, that we are all brothers and sisters, and are all responsible for each other, put into effect – and that does not extend to Muslims alone, but to non-Muslims and the creatures of this earth. We have a major task ahead of us, and that is protecting our earth and surviving.'

The Hostages and Islam

But where, as the saying has it, is the beef? What *will* correct the prejudices of the outsider, far more even than Muslims speaking for themselves and in their own words, will be the concerted action or protest of Muslims against what *they themselves* insist is a contradiction of Islam. To take one specific example: the Qur'ān and Sharia give careful rules for the conduct of war and the treatment of prisoners of war. As a result there is no doubt of any kind whatsoever, that the taking of hostages in the Lebanon, however understandable the anger and frustration, was a total contradiction of those rules and thus of Islam – as these speakers, interviewed while the hostages were still in captivity, made clear:

'I think Islam is very clear on this issue, and in my opinion Islam does not allow the taking of hostages where a war has not been declared. In the case of war, that is a different situation. But if, as a community, we have not declared war, we are not allowed to make hostages of civilians. Now I think that in the Lebanon we are dealing with a very abnormal situation. Though I may not agree with the taking of hostages in the Lebanon, at least I can understand why this has occurred. I think that the rest of the world has got to understand why this has occurred, so that it does not happen again, and so that the hostages who have been taken can be released as quickly as possible. We are dealing with people who are under extreme pressure, under great human degradation, and for them it is the only way to bring the world's attention to their particular problem. No matter what our personal prejudice may be, we have to come to terms with this. However, as far as Islam and the Sharia is concerned, unless war has been declared, we are not allowed to take hostages in this way.'

JB: 'Should there be marches of protest, or letters of protest, that are not just Muslim? Is this the kind of issue where you would hope to see joint action among Muslims, Jews, Christians, Buddhists, humanists, atheists – co-operation, in other words, in saying that the taking of hostages is a contradiction of Islam?'

'I think that is correct. It is not only a contradiction of Islam, it is a contradiction of human existence. None of us can tolerate this. It is for all religious communities, since they are all concerned with the value of human life, to work together and come together to try to resolve this particular issue. To allow this to continue does not contribute to peace.'

'"Protest" may of course be the wrong word, since that might itself be a contradiction of the Islamic preference for discussion, debate and advice. But that would not affect the perception that the taking of these hostages was unequivocally wrong – from an Islamic point of view.'

'We do not call it "protestation", we rather call it "advice", because it has to be given, not in animosity, but in love and affection and concern. Sometimes we do things publicly, when it is required, but more often we do it quietly. We write and protest about a lot of things which concern people in this country [UK]; for example, concerning the hostages, we write and express our views. Most certainly the taking of hostages is contrary to the legislation on the treatment of prisoners. For a start, some of the hostages are not even prisoners of war at all. They should not be taken as hostages at all, because their only crime is that they hold a particular passport. Some of them are Muslims, by the way. How could you, as a Muslim, take a Muslim hostage? But these are activities of groups who do not represent Islam in its real meaning or application. It is a community beleaguered, frightened. It is abhorrent, it is horrible and it is objectionable. But no one has ever queried Reagan, sending his huge battleship and bombarding villages of innocent people who have committed nothing whatsoever, no one has ever questioned the Israelis sending their aeroplanes and blindly blanketing areas with bombs and killing innocent people. Nobody says anything

161

about these things at all, because they are just dispensable Muslims, but if it is just one European, then you get all the hullabaloo in the West. If the West would actually measure things equally, talk about things from a principle, and not from a skewed outlook, then I think they would be listened to more.

'But as for myself, I objected. In fact, I tell you that when the American hostages were taken in Tehran, I made a statement there and then, and I wrote about it, saying that these were ambassadors, and ambassadors are protected under Muslim law. We said this, not to support the Americans, but only to stand for the principles of Islam. We have appealed for the release of hostages in the Lebanon. By the way, let me remind you that Muslim hostages were taken by the Falange. It was the Falange who started the whole taking of hostages in the Lebanon, not the Muslims. But no one mentions those hundreds of hostages – at least four hundred hostages were taken by the Falange, but nobody mentions them because, again, they were dispensable Muslims. The rule for Islam is that it is wrong to take hostages. Those people were not combatants. Many of them were university teachers or aid workers or correspondents. If you do not have a specific accusation against a person as aiding the military action against the community, you have no justification whatsoever.'

There is no mistaking the pain underlying that statement. The extreme unevenness of the West in relation to Israel and the Arabs has undoubtedly created a wretched desperation, which is not alleviated by saying that the Arabs should have made wiser decisions in 1917 or 1947. Nevertheless, the dignity of Islam still comes through. And for a religion that writes its history *bismillahi rahmani warahim*, in the name of God, the merciful, the compassionate (the opening words of the Qur'ān), it would have been a mark of new hope for the future if there had been a more public *Muslim* protest (on Muslim grounds) against the taking and keeping of innocent hostages.

For Islam is a religion which lives towards a horizon of hope. Its voice is a powerful reinforcement – or could be – in making sense of the new circumstance which the technological and population revolutions have created; a circumstance in which the former creates and the latter demands transnational and transcendental co-operation:

'We are all part of one another, whether we like it or not. Someone may think, "Oh! I can't stand him!" But he is on this earth as much as I am on this earth. We have got to find ways of bridging chasms of misunderstanding, because we have this thing called the earth, which is at the moment in perilous danger. From the Muslim point of view, man was put on this earth as God's trustee, as His vice-regent – that's a rather archaic translation of *khalifa*, but I think we know what it means. It means that we do not own the land or possess it in order to consume it. We are trustees for future generations. In fact one of the earliest of the Caliphs, one of the Guided Caliphs, advised the umma when it was going to war – which was quite frequent in the early years – not to attack women, children and civilians, not to destroy sources of water or fruit-bearing trees, in other words, to limit destruction to the very minimum. That's a part of the whole role of being a trustee of the fruits of the earth. In this we have the germs of our responsibility to the earth and to our fellow human beings.'

JB: 'But why should I do something for future generations? As someone has said: what are future generations going to do for me?'

'That's a Lewis Carroll question! When you have a child, you are expressing, objectively, an idea of hope. Objectively, it is an idea of hope.'

Postscript

The voices of Islam in this book are far removed from the popular perceptions of Islam with which we began. They are mainly calm and inclusive; they are, generally speaking, tolerant, and they are quite prepared to engage in vigorous internal arguments with each other. How, then, has the very different impression of Islam come about?

In part, it is a consequence of the centuries of Western expansion and imperialism, and of the realignment of subsequent ideologies and economic strengths; and in conjunction with all that, it is a consequence also of the protective nature of religions as cultural systems. Like all religions, Islam is a strongly bounded information system – to put the matter technically – and that observation has large consequences. In my books *Licensed Insanities: Religions and Belief in God in the Contemporary World* and *Is God a Virus? Genes, Culture and Religion*, I have tried to show how all religions are organized to protect and transmit (from one life or from one generation to another) information which human communities have found true and valuable through extremely long periods of history. Religions are the earliest cultural systems of which we have any evidence that enhance the chances of survival. *Of course* there is much more going on in developed religious communities than that. But unless we understand the baseline of religions as long-running systems to protect information which has been identified (or simply accepted) as constitutive of worth and value and truth, then we will never understand why religious people (and especially the leaders to whom the responsibility accrues of maintaining the system and thus of protecting the information which they have inherited) are so often intransigent and always conservative. All systems have boundaries, whether literal (for example, in terms of geography) or metaphorical. Where you have boundaries, there you will predictably have border incidents, whenever anyone, or any group of people, feels that their boundary is under threat; and again, the threat may be literal or metaphorical (in terms of conceptual or actual invasion). Equally, strong systems have strong internal logics or emotions which press towards totalitarian imperialism: Vatican Catholicism is a consistent example of this truth, and so are some versions of Islam at the present time.

I have stated all this in over-simplified form. We could make it more rigorous by talking about the primacy of gene-replication and the nurture of children in the determination of cultural form (and that is why religions 'lock on to' sex and food in so basic a way); we could remind ourselves that 'information' includes much more than verbal items (and that in the case of religions the non-verbal is profoundly and extensively important); and we could investigate how it comes about that the conditions governing the information process create the vastly different forms and styles of the different religions by virtue of being systems. And some of these details are in my book, mentioned above. Here it is enough – I hope – to keep it over-simple in order to alert a world, which has largely ceased in its secular versions to understand religion or to take it seriously in any way at all, to what is more truly and fundamentally at issue. The more that religions are regarded as private options which some rather weak-minded people take up in their spare time instead of fishing or football, the more their defensive behaviours under threat will be written off as fanaticism. Religions are only so dangerous because they are so important.

They are the source of virtually everything that humans have come to regard as important and valuable – art, architecture, dance, drama, poetry, hope, vision, compassion – as well as making mind-extending discoveries of what this human architecture of atoms and molecules is capable of being and becoming; and yes, they have come to the sense also, not of discovering, but of being discovered by God. It is because so much is protected, secured and transmitted through religious systems that people in those systems are capable of such horrific and 'fundamentalistically' zealous behaviours.

To say all that does not confer automatic truth on everything that any religious person happens to say, even if one is evaluating truth within the logic of the system concerned. Obviously not. Issues of truth are truly the point in question, within a religion, between religions, and between religious and non-religious views. But the chances of any serious engagement with such issues of truth are totally destroyed by those who approach religion with the prejudgement (i.e. prejudice) that it is trivial and not a subject worthy of academic attention (apparently the opinion of Mr Kenneth Baker, while Secretary of State for Education, when interviewed once on radio) or that it is odious.

That last word comes from the opening sentence of a review of books about 'the Rushdie affair' in the *Independent*: 'It is very easy to yield to the temptation of high-mindedness when discussing the Rushdie affair: to talk about the gulf of misunderstanding separating two great traditions of civilization when what we actually mean is that Islam strikes us as a completely odious religion.' But that is not the Islam described in this book. What is described here is the Islam of history, which rescued Greek science and philosophy for the world, under which Jews were a great deal safer than they were under

Christians in Europe, which defends a vision of human community as its most fundamental enabling concept, and all the rest, all the many points made in this book.

Certainly that history contains horror and outrage, as will its present practice, human beings being what they are. Thus on the day that this page was being typed, it was reported that a professor of biology at Khartoum University had been imprisoned, beaten and tortured for teaching evolution. Such things cannot be reconciled with Islam, even though they are done by those who have no doubt that they are Muslims. The point is that Muslims themselves have their legitimate grounds of protest against such things – legitimized, that is, in the Qur'ān itself – and in the case of the report from Sudan, that protest was made (by one of the contributors to this book) in no uncertain terms: 'The authorities must have gone completely mad . . . I don't see any contradiction between Darwin's theory and Islam. The Qur'ān is neutral as far as biological arguments are concerned.' So while undoubtedly it will remain the case that beliefs and practices will continue which seem abhorrent and false, they will seem so not only to non-Muslims, but often to Muslims as well. But more important by far are the immense and many virtues in Islam which could be far more effectively mobilized if they were given the support which – disastrously – the post-religiously educated generation of the Western world seems incapable of giving.

Is all this special pleading? No. There is nothing stated in this book which does not have its authentic and legitimizing warrant within Islam itself. These are voices of Islam which are not odious. They point to the ways in which Islam can recover its confidence, not as a threat to the outsider, but as a reinforcement of those actions which the many threats to the planet seem to be demanding of us all. If Islam in practice at the present time seems to be different from the Islam which this book describes, the wiser response would be to reinforce those Muslims who speak with the voices of this book, not to increase the pressures which exacerbate defensive responses.

We live in an unexpected and surprising era, in which the errors of the dominant voices of cultural relativism and subjectivity have been revealed. The necessity is urgent upon us to transcend the nation-state and to find not merely international but transnational voices, whether one is thinking of ecology, drugs, corporations, trade, high-cost scientific research, chemical weapons, or now, of morality and value. The vocabularies of such discourse will not be found in the platitudes of most current international conferences – especially those of religions, where such highly funded organizations as the Global Forum meet extravagantly to vote against pollution and sin. In contrast, we do have *some* precedents and wisdom to guide us. The very different ways in which two large and culturally diverse collections of people sought to attach the word 'united' to 'states of America', and 'union' to 'soviet socialist republics', have much to teach us in both directions – both how and how not to go about it. And there are other precedents: India is one; the Commonwealth could still be another despite the abject way in which the United (another precedent?) Kingdom abandoned the experiment.

For the sake of human community and human good (about which we no longer have to capitulate to the relativists), we should welcome and endorse and reinforce the voices of Islam which are the majority of voices in this book. There will remain that which the non-Muslim will contest and dislike in the Muslim world, just as there will be that which Muslims dislike and contest in the non-Muslim world. But the context of that attention to truth will be entirely different; and the protest of both non-Muslim and Muslim together, where it is appropriate, will have far more chance of being the agent of God's work in 'turning the wicked from their ways' and of bearing in hands of mercy the oppressed and the hungry of the earth.

Glossary

Abbasids: (Arab.: *ad-dawlah al-'abbasiyyah*) second Muslim dynasty (after the Umayyads, see below), in power from AH 132–656/CE 749–1258. Their name is derived from their ancestor, al-'Abbas, the uncle of the Prophet Muhammad. Under the Abbasids, Arab-Islamic civilization reached great heights.

adhan: call to prayer, hence *mu'adhin* (muezzin), the one who calls to prayer.

AH: Anno Hegirae, or more usually, After the Hijra, the abbreviation for the numbering of years in the Muslim calendar. The Hijra was the move by Muhammad from Mecca to Medina in the year 622 (according to the Christian calendar). From this year Muslim years are counted. Since the Muslim months are lunar, the years do not synchronize with the solar calculations. For tables of correspondence, see G. S. P. Freeman-Grenville's *The Muslim and Christian Calendars* (Oxford University Press, 1963).

ahl al-Kitab: 'The People of the Book': *al-Kitab* is the Qur'ān, and *ahl al-Kitab* are those whom the Qur'ān designates as having received God's revelation in the past. In ii. 58, cf. v. 69, they are described as

171

Jews, Christians and those of the Sabians who believe in God and the Last Day. They have a special status in relation to Muslims. Since the Qur'ān speaks of every nation as having received its messenger (x. 47, xl. 78), it is an issue, discussed in this book, whether there are more 'peoples of the Book', and if so, who they are.

alim, ulama: (Arab.: *'alim,* pl. *'ulama*) a learned person, one who is recognized as an authority in religious matters. The ulama have an independence from political authority, whatever form that may take. Thus in the past they formally elected a sovereign as ruler. Their role, especially as imams and judges, has been to monitor the life of the community in relation to the received tradition of Islam. For some Shia Muslims, the ulama may have an even higher status, able to make autonomous legal decisions, and they often have a personal following as *Ayat-Allah* ('a sign of God'), i.c. as ayatollahs.

aya (pl. *ayat*): 'a sign' or 'a mark', in the Qur'ān, a mark of God's existence and power (ii. 248, iii. 41, xxvi. 197, etc.) and especially a miracle. The greatest sign and miracle of God is the Qur'ān itself, and sections of the Qur'ān shorter than suras (the major 'chapter' divisions of the Qur'ān) are referred to as *ayat* (e.g. ii. 99, iii. 58 and 164, xxviii. 87, xlv. 5). From this usage, the word has come to mean the verses of the Qur'ān.

172

ayatollah: *see alim.*

Caliph: (Arab.: *khalifa*) 'successor', 'representative'. In ii.
30, Adam, as the one who embodies the *fitra*
(human nature as God intended it, see below), is
called the Caliph of God, i.e. His agent or
representative on earth. Muhammad is often
regarded as the Caliph of God in this sense; the
subsequent Caliphs are his successors as the
spiritual and temporal leaders of the Islamic state.

darajah: 'rank' or 'degree', the relation of husbands to
their wives according to ii. 228.

dhimmi: an individual who belongs to *ahl adh-Dhimma*, the
people of protected status – generally speaking,
members of *ahl al-Kitab* (see above). They had
particular privileges, and although they
remained clearly second-class citizens, they
could, and often did, rise to high positions in
administration and finance, and in medicine.

din: 'lifeway', often translated as 'religion', though *din*
embraces much more than the English word
'religion' usually represents. Islam is called *din al-
haqq* (the way of truth, xxviii. 28, lxi. 9), and
Islam is often summarized as *din wa-dawla*, i.e.
'religion-and-state', since there is no distinction
between religion and politics. It is likely that *din*
is related to *daina*, 'debt', with the implication of
obligation; thus *din* represents the duties of faith
and practice, and also the debt or account to be

paid, hence *Yaum ud-Din*, the Day of Judgement.

fatwa: a legal opinion given on request to an individual or to a public body or institution (e.g. a magistrate) concerning a doubtful point of law. One qualified to give an opinion is a *mufti*, and his decision accords with a particular *madhab* (school of law). It is not an infallible pronouncement, and is sifted by reception according to existing precedents.

fiqh: jurisprudence, the science of religious law in Islam. Originally it meant understanding of the law ordained by God, i.e. Sharia, in conjunction with Kalam, the science of theology. Four major schools of law emerged, now known as the Hanbalite, Hanifite, Malikite and Shafiite (Shiites and Kharijites have their own schools). One who studies *fiqh* is known as a *faqih*. The four accepted foundations of *fiqh* are Qur'ān, Hadith, *qiyas* and *ijma'*.

fitra: human nature as intended by God in its moral and religious disposition. Its fundamental importance in the Muslim understanding of human nature rests on xxx. 30: 'Set your face to the *din* [see above] as a *hanif* [one who follows the monotheistic faith and practice of Abraham], the nature of God on which He natured humankind.' This is usually taken to mean that human nature is designed and intended for Islam. But some commentators take it to mean

that humans are by nature Muslim, and that it is
parents who make children other than Muslim.

Hadith: 'speech', 'narrative', the collected record of the
acts, words and silences of Muhammad and his
companions. A Hadith consists of two parts,
matn (text) and *isnad* (chain of transmission). An
elaborate science of Hadith grew up to assess
and classify the Hadith in relation to their
authenticity.

hajj: pilgrimage, in particular the pilgrimage to
Mecca and specifically to the Ka'ba. It is one of
the five pillars of Islam. See chapter 1.

halal: 'released from prohibition', i.e. that which is
lawful in Islam; it applies especially to food,
hence halal meat, that which has been
slaughtered according to the ritual laws.

haram: 'restricted', 'forbidden', that which is unlawful in
Islam. By extension, the word also applies to that
which is sacred, especially holy places.

hijab: any partition which separates two things (i.e.
that which separates God from His creation),
but usually the veil worn by Muslim women.
The Qur'ān commands modesty in dress (xxiv.
31), for men as for women, but does not specify
the detail. The extent of the covering is disputed
and varies from country to country. The almost
complete covering by the *chador* is not a

specific requirement of the Qur'ān.

ijma':   'assembly', the consensus of Muslims, especially
            the ulama, on a question of law. Ijma is one of
            the four accepted *usul al-Fiqh*, the principles of
            fiqh (see above), which extends the
            interpretation of law. It rests on the Hadith,
            'My people will never agree in error'.

ijtihad: 'effort', the fourth of the foundations of *fiqh* (see
            above). A person who is qualified to make the
            application of known law to new situations is
            known as a *mujtahid*. Among Sunnis, there is
            some reluctance to allow *ijtihad*, since it is
            supposed to rest on a perfect knowledge of all
            established law. However, it rests on a Hadith in
            which Muhammad asks Mu'az by what criteria
            he will administer judicial decisions. 'Mu'az
            replied, "By the Qur'ān." "Then what?" "By the
            Sunna." "Then what?" "Then I will make a
            personal effort and act on that basis." And the
            Prophet approved of that.' Among Shia Muslims,
            ijtihad has a more prominent role.

ilm: (Arab.: *'ilm*) knowledge of all kinds, but
            especially of *fiqh* and Kalam. See *fiqh*.

imam: 'sign', 'pattern', 'leader', the leader of Muslim
            congregational prayer. He must be a man of
            good standing in the community, and is often
            theologically educated and engaged by the
            mosque; but there is no 'ordination', so he does

not resemble the Christian priest: he is only
imam while acting as such. Among Shia
Muslims, the imam has an incomparably higher
status, since the imam, as the rightful successor
of 'Alī, receives and transmits divine guidance.

iman: 'be secure', 'trust', faith and trust, especially in
God and in the Prophet Muhammad.

intifada: 'uprising', the name given to the Palestinian
revolt which began in December 1987, in Gaza
and on the West Bank.

jihad: (Arab.: *jahd,* 'effort') making an effort on behalf
of God, *jihad fi sabil Allah.* The greater jihad is the
warfare in oneself against evil and temptation.
The lesser jihad is warfare in the defence of a
Muslim country or community. A person who
engages in the lesser jihad is known as a
mujahid.

juma: (Arab.: *salat al-Jum'ah*) the Friday midday prayer
performed in a congregational mosque (lxii. 9).
It is obligatory for free, adult males. Women
may attend, but will be strictly separated from
men; it is held to be a mercy from God that they
are excused this obligation.

kafir: an unbeliever, one who rejects God and His
messenger. The offence is *kufr.*

khalifa: *see Caliph.*

mahr:
dowry, the gift from the groom which remains the bride's property. She keeps all of it in the case of divorce, half of it if the marriage is dissolved before consummation.

masjid:
(Arab.: *sajada*, 'he bowed down, prostrated himself') the place of prostration, i.e. a mosque.

mujahid:
see *jihad*.

mujtahid:
see *ijtihad*.

mushrik:
see *shirk*.

qiyas:
'measure', reaching a conclusion about an unknown point of law by analogy. It is one of the four accepted foundations of *fiqh* (see above).

Qur'ān:
(Arab.: *al-Qur'ān*) 'the reading' or 'the recitation', the revelations from God transmitted through Muḥammad and now collected together. Since every nation has received its prophet (see *ahl al-Kitab* above), the essential content of the Qur'ān has been revealed many times, but only in the case of the Arabs has the revelation been preserved without corruption.

Ramadan:
the ninth month of the Muslim calendar during which a dawn to dusk fast is kept.

riba:
(Arab.: *raba*, 'grow', 'increase') profit obtained by

way of interest on the loan of money or goods,
and as such forbidden.

Shahada: (Arab., *ash-Shahada*) the witness, the first of the
five pillars of Islam: 'I bear witness that there is
no God but God, and that Muhammad is His
apostle.'

Sharia: (Arab.: *shari'a*) 'the well-worn path to the
watering place', the prescribed path which
Muslims follow in their lives. The term goes
back to the Qur'ān (i.e. xlv. 18, 'We gave you a
religion, so follow it...'), but it now means, more
usually, the formal working out of the allowed
and the forbidden (halal and haram, see above)
in the schools of Islamic law, established on the
basis of the Qur'ān, the Sunna, *qiyas* and *ijma'*.

Shiites: those who belong to *shi'atu 'Alī*, the party of 'Alī;
they are approximately ten per cent of all
Muslims. See chapter 1.

shirk: 'association', the worst of sins in Islam, the
association (i.e. making equal) with God of that
which is not God.

shura: assembly; forms of collective consultation and
decision-making.

Sūfism: (Arab.: *at-tassawuf*; etymology uncertain, possibly
from *suf*, 'wool', from the characteristic woollen
garment worn by Sūfīs; or *ahl as-suffa*, the people

sitting on 'the bench' of the mosque at Medina;
or *sufiyya*, those who have been purified, etc.)
Those who gain experiential knowledge of the
interior truths of Islam, often called 'mystics'.
Although they are sometimes contrasted with
Muslims who follow Sharia, this is a mistake, as
the two coexist and represent the interior and
exterior requirements of true faith and practice.

Sunna: 'custom', the customary observances of any
people or nation, but more usually, the spoken
and acted example of the Prophet Muhammad.
As the first living exemplar of Islam, and the
bearer of God's revelation, his words and deeds
became one of the four foundations of *fiqh* (see
above). This is enjoined in the Qur'ān itself, 'You
have a good example in the messenger of God'
(xxxiii. 21).

Sunnis: those who follow the example and keep the
customs of Muhammad, as these are embedded
in *fiqh*. They form the majority, about eighty-five
per cent, of Muslims (see also Shiites above).
Their full name is *ahl as-sunnah wa-l-ijma*, the
people of the sunna and the consensus.

sura: see *aya*.

talaq: the proclamation of divorce. See chapter 4.

tawhid: (Arab.: *wahhada*, 'make one') the unity of God,
the affirmation of which is the supreme duty and

delight of Muslim life. Sura cxii, the Sura of
Unity, is the classic statement.

ulama: *see alim.*

Umayyads: (Arab.: *ad-dawlah al-umawiyyah*) the first Muslim
dynasty after the *ar-Rashidun* (the upright ones,
the four immediate successors of Muḥammad as
Caliphs). It lasted from AH 41/CE 661 to
132/750. It became notorious for its tyranny and
self-interest.

umma: people or community; it underlies the
fundamental Muslim sense of all people being
intended to be a single umma under God.

zakat: (Arab.: *zakah*, understood as purification) the
giving up of a portion of one's wealth (in excess
of what is needed for sustenance) to purify (i.e.
legitimize) what remains. It is often translated as
'tithe', and it is one of the five pillars of Islam.

Index

Pakistan, 13, 26, 57, 88, 113, 115, 122, 132
Palestine, 76, 88
paradise, 34, 50
People of the Book (*ahl al-Kitab*), 19, 20, 21, 90–2, 94, 97, 98, 99, 128, 171–2, 173
persecution, 87, 113, 116
pilgrimage (*hajj*), *see* five pillars of Islam
Plato, 159
polygamy, 131–3
polytheism, 98
population, 36
prayer, 17, 30, 36, 141, 177; *see also* five pillars of Islam
Prideaux, Humphrey, 15, 107
Prophet, the, *see* Muḥammad
prophets, 21, 31, 47, 90, 91, 115, 151, 178: prophetic tradition, 26–7
protest, Muslim, 71–2, 134–5, 158–63, 168

qadi, 134
qadr, 32
qawwumun, 125, 126
qiyas, 26, 51, 174, 178, 179
Quasem, M. A., 10
Qur'ān, 10, 15, 17, 18, 19, 20–1,22, 26–7, 28, 31, 34, 40, 41, 51, 52, 54, 58, 59, 60, 64, 65–6, 70, 72, 76, 80, 83, 84, 85, 86, 89, 90, 91, 92, 93, 96, 99, 100, 104, 105, 110, 111, 114, 116, 117, 118, 124, 125, 126, 128, 129, 130, 131, 132–3, 137, 138, 139–42, 148, 151, 152, 154, 155–6, 157, 160, 162, 168, 171–2, 174, 175, 176, 178, 179: commentaries, 48, 136, 143; exegesis

and interpretation, 20, 22, 23, 43–50, 70, 99–100, 102, 125, 126–7, 131, 157

Ramadan, 178
Reagan, Ronald, 161
revelation, 20–1, 36, 37, 40, 43, 63, 64, 65, 73, 90, 91, 97, 154, 155, 171, 178
riba, 43–4, 51, 52–6, 178
Rushdie, Salman, 13, 24, 69, 72, 80, 101–2, 105, 106, 107, 109, 110–12, 113, 114, 157, 167: *The Satanic Verses*, 9, 13, 101, 105–13, 159

sabb, 106
Saddam Hussein, *see* Hussein, Saddam
Satan, 102
Saudi Arabia, 18, 25, 26, 35, 77, 95, 96, 97, 122, 124
secularism, 32, 143, 150–2
self-control, 18
seven articles of faith, 30, 31–2
Shafii, 83, 124
Shafiites, 174
Shahada, see five pillars of Islam
Sharia (*shari'a*), 10, 21–2, 23, 26, 33, 37, 40, 41, 42, 52, 53, 56, 57, 58, 71, 74, 79, 82, 124, 134, 135–6, 137, 141, 142, 149, 160, 174, 179, 180: interpretation of, 50–2, 116, 136, 158; schools of, 22, 51, 70, 124, 158, 174
shatin, 106
Shia (*shi'a*), 23, 24, 25, 26, 67, 72, 111, 172, 176
Shiism, 73
Shiites, 23, 24, 174, 179
shirk, 92, 99, 179

shura, 66, 68, 179
Sikhs, 18
sin, *see* original sin
Spain, 15, 17, 90, 151, 155
state: Islamic, 38, 39, 40, 57, 72–3,
  74, 77, 80, 82, 95, 105, 110,
  112, 138, 173; Muslim, 40, 66,
  68–9, 74–5, 83, 84; nation-
  state, 17, 68, 69, 75, 77, 78,
  105, 169
Sudan, 13, 168
Sūfism, 49, 179–80
Sunna, 21–2, 26, 27, 33, 40, 51,
  80, 117, 140, 141, 143, 176,
  179, 180
Sunni(s), 23, 25, 26, 67, 72, 111,
  176, 180
Sunnism, 73
systems, religions as, 165–6

talaq, *see* divorce
tawhid, 77, 92, 180
tolerance, 19–20, 40, 57, 89
Tradition, 58, 59, 63, 71, 100, 104,
  121, 136; *see also* Hadith
Trinity, 93
Tunisia, 132
Turkey, 18, 55

Uhud, battle of, 65
ulama (*'ulama*), 23, 27–8, 51, 53,
  54, 63, 73, 96, 98, 132, 140,
  172, 176
Umar, 27, 44
Umayyads, 38, 136, 171, 181
umma, 17, 22, 26, 68, 69, 75,
  76–7, 78, 79–80, 105, 110,
  113, 159, 163, 181; *see also*

community
unIslamic activities, 54, 110
United Kingdom, 29, 38–9, 89,
  97, 106, 110, 112, 132, 134,
  137, 138–9, 145, 147, 148,
  161, 169
United Nations, 84
'urubiyya, *see* Arabism

values, 144–5
Vedas, 98
veil, *see hijab*

war, 41, 74, 81–2, 83–4, 84–9,
  114, 160, 161, 163, 177; *see also*
  jihad
women, 119–36: and adultery, 58,
  62; and apostasy, 101; beating
  of wives, 128–31; changing
  attitudes to, 38, 136; circumcision of, 71; dress, 14, 121–4,
  175; education of, 135,
  148–50; equality of, 121, 124,
  149; men and, 119–20, 124–34;
  polygamy, 131–3; property
  rights, 122, 128, 135; rights of,
  62, 134–6; segregation of, 149,
  177; subordination of, 9, 16,
  118, 120, 123; 'traditional' role
  of, 14, 121
World Conference on Muslim
  Education, 142

Yemen, 103

zakat, *see* five pillars of Islam
Zia-ul-Haq, 113
Zoroastrians, 40

188